How to make
sales
when you don't like
selling

Other books about running a small business from How To Books

WAKE UP AND SMELL THE PROFIT
52 guaranteed ways to make more money in your coffee business
John Richardson and Hugh Gilmartin

THE SMALL BUSINESS START-UP WORKBOOK
A step-by-step guide to starting the business you've dreamed of
Cheryl D Rickman

PREPARE TO SELL YOUR COMPANY
A guide to planning and implementing a successful exit
L B Buckingham

WRITE YOUR OWN BUSINESS PLAN
A step-by-step guide to building a plan that will secure finance and transform your business
Paul Hetherington

SETTING UP AND RUNNING A LIMITED COMPANY
A comprehensive guide to forming and operating a company as a director and shareholder
Robert Browning

Write or phone for a catalogue to:

How To Books
Spring Hill House
Spring Hill Road
Begbroke
Oxford
OX5 1RX
Tel. 01865 375794

Or email: info@howtobooks.co.uk

Visit our website www.howtobooks.co.uk
to find out more about us and our books

Like us on Facebook page **How To Books & Spring Hill**

Follow us on Twitter **@Howtobooksltd**

Read our books online www.howto.co.uk

How to make sales

when you don't like

selling

ALAN FAIRWEATHER

howtobooks

Published by How To Books Ltd,
Spring Hill House, Spring Hill Road,
Begbroke, Oxford OX5 1RX
Tel: (01865) 375794. Fax: (01865) 379162
info@howtobooks.co.uk
www.howtobooks.co.uk

How To Books greatly reduce the carbon footprint of their books by sourcing their
typesetting and printing in the UK.

British Library Cataloguing in Publication Data
A catalogue record for this book is available from the British Library

ISBN: 978 1 84528 479 4

Cover design by Baseline Arts Ltd, Oxford
Produced for How To Books by Deer Park Productions, Tavistock, Devon
Typeset by PDQ Typesetting, Newcastle-under-Lyme, Staffs.
Printed and bound in Great Britain by Bell & Bain Ltd, Glasgow

NOTE: The material contained in this book is set out in good faith for general guidance
and no liability can be accepted for loss or expense incurred as a result of relying in
particular circumstances on statements made in the book. Laws and regulations are
complex and liable to change, and readers should check the current position with the
relevant authorities before making personal arrangements.

Contents

Preface

Selling is tough! Making sales is one of the hardest jobs there is. Why? Because the majority of people will tell you they don't need your product or service, don't want it, and can't afford it. And there's no stock answer to that; no magic bullet that will turn a non-customer into a customer. However, if you are a small business owner or a sole trader, then you must find new clients and customers. You need to make sales to ensure your business survives, and is profitable and successful.

As a modern businessperson, you need to develop skills, knowledge, attitude and personal qualities to meet the greater expectations of your customers and their business.

This book addresses the qualities, knowledge and skills needed by a professional businessperson. It is primarily directed at those who have not been trained in sales, and are not particularly comfortable about selling. It examines the importance of attitude, sales psychology and basic sales techniques. It will show you how to get customers to *come to you* and motivate them to buy.

Once you have worked through this book you will have a better understanding of why people buy; how to be more proactive, influence decisions, become more persuasive and build lasting customer relationships.

> *Unless the man who works in an office is able to sell himself and his ideas, unless he has the power to convince others of the soundness of his convictions, he can never achieve his goal. He may have the best ideas in the world; he may have plans which would revolutionize entire industries. But unless he can persuade others that his ideas are good, he will never get the chance to put*

them into effect. Stripped of non-essentials, all business activity is a sales battle. And everyone in business must be a salesman.

Robert E.M. Cowie

Keeping It Simple

'GET OUT – STAY OUT – AND DON'T COME BACK'

This was the punchline to a joke a heard a few years ago. The question from the wife to her salesman husband was:

'Did you get any orders today darling?'

'Yes I did; I got three orders – "Get out – stay out – and don't come back!"'

This is often the image people have of salespeople. Someone who is trying to *sell* a product or service to another person who doesn't want it, doesn't need it, and can't afford it.

We tend to have a negative view about salespeople. They're not exactly up there with the doctors, lawyers, engineers, accountants and other professionals. They are often not even in the same league as tradespeople such as plumbers, carpenters or electricians.

It is rare for someone to describe themselves as a salesman or saleswoman. They usually describe themselves as sales executives, sales managers or sales engineers.

Every time I run a sales seminar for businesspeople I ask the group how they feel about sales and selling. They come back with comments such as:

- 'It's something you've got to do.'

- 'I hate making cold calls.'

- 'I hate receiving cold calls.'

- 'Salespeople can be really annoying.'

- 'You've got to be a good talker.'

- 'You need to be able to manipulate people.'

- 'If you don't put on the pressure then you won't get the sale.'

- 'I'm not really a salesperson.'

There are many more comments like this, and it may not surprise you to know that they all tend to be a bit negative about selling and salespeople.

Because of this negativity, many businesspeople can feel a bit uncomfortable about selling their product or service. They don't want to be seen as pushy or annoying to a potential customer. Human beings have a huge fear of rejection. We just hate to hear the word 'No!' We will do almost anything to avoid rejection. And of course, fear of rejection stops people contacting customers, asking for an order, or some other form of commitment.

It's fairly normal and understandable to feel this way, particularly if selling is not what you were trained to do. Occasionally I do some electrical work around the house or even some mechanical work on the car. However, it's not what I trained to do, so I can get a bit uncomfortable, particularly when it starts to go wrong (electric shocks and bruised fingers are not unknown to me).

But you need to find a way round all this if you are to have a successful business.

What do you need?

What everyone wants to know is – 'What does it take to succeed in business? Is it a great product or service, or perhaps plenty of money or even modern premises and dedicated staff?'

All of these are great but what you really need are customers.

Whether you want a small business or a big business, you need customers. You might not like cold calling and selling your product or service, but you *do* need new customers and lots of them.

Achieving the right mindset

You might be thinking – 'I have customers and as long as I keep them happy things will be OK.' I hate to tell you, but no matter how good your product or service is, you *will* lose customers. They'll either leave the area, or they'll die, or they'll go out of business themselves, or just decide to deal with somebody else. So you need to find new customers just to stand still. However, that's not what you bought this book for – you want to find lots and lots of customers. To do that you've got to get in the right mindset; you've got to think like a successful *marketer*.

Every day you need to allocate time to marketing and selling your product or service. Do not fall into the trap of saying, 'I'll do it tomorrow, I'm too busy today.' Overall, you need to spend about 20% of your time on marketing and selling.

There are many failed businesses that had a fantastic product or service. However, the majority failed because they didn't spend enough time marketing and selling. That is not going to happen to you, so let's keep going.

FINDING CLIENTS AND CUSTOMERS

There are two ways of finding clients and customers.

1. You get them to come to *you* and buy your product or service.

2. You go to *them* and sell them your product or service.

You might be absolutely brilliant at working in your business, or at providing your service, or manufacturing and supplying your product. But if you want to remain in business, then you are going to have to take action on point 1 or point 2 and *preferably both*.

You may have a business where customers beat a path to your door. However, the day may come when they no longer tread that path, and they may even beat a path to your competitor's door. So there's no escaping the selling business. The first president of IBM, Thomas J. Watson Sr, once said: 'Nothing happens in this company until somebody sells something.'

In other words, you can build the most fantastic computers in the world, but until someone gets out there and sells them, then you don't have a business.

Successful businesspeople realize that the selling business has changed over the years, and embrace that change. Sadly, there are still many businesspeople still living in the past.

We're going to explore point 1 and I'll show you how to get customers to come to you. We will then examine the sales process and I'll give you practical tools you can use. Let's consider why people buy anything, whether it's for themselves or their business.

UNDERSTANDING WHY PEOPLE BUY

I was running a seminar for staff at a health and fitness club and I asked them 'What do you think are the reasons people decide to join a health club?' The answers came back:

- to lose weight;

- to get fitter;

- to have a better shape;

- to build muscles;

- because they like swimming.

These answers are all perfectly valid, but there a whole host of other reasons why people would want to join a health club, including the following:

- to meet other people;

- to find a new partner;

- to be able to say, 'I go to a health club';

- because they like the music in the aerobic classes;

- to feel they belong;

- it's the thing to do;

- to sleep better;

- to have more energy;

- to have a sharper mind.

There are lots of reasons why people could buy your product or service, and you need to be aware what they are or could be.

People buy to solve either real or perceived problems. They want to move away from pain and towards pleasure. They want to feel better after having made the decision to buy your product or service than they did before. So it follows that *buying decisions are emotional.*

USING YOUR HEART OR YOUR HEAD

All decisions to buy are emotional because people are driven by their emotions in everything they say and do.

We buy religion and politics, and we buy other people based on our emotions. We also buy products and services based on emotions.

People will decide to buy emotionally and then justify logically. Picture the man who buys a new Mercedes instead of a basic family car, and then tries to justify the extra cost to his partner. He'll explain all about the reliable German engineering, the superb after-sales service and the high resale value. However, as we all know, he probably bought the Mercedes to impress the neighbours and his friends. It was another decision based on emotions.

Some people will also buy a house (probably their most expensive purchase) because they feel good about it.

Discovering what customers won't always tell you

Your customers won't always tell you the real reason for buying your product or service. Take my example of the health and fitness club – a potential new member might tell you that they want to lose weight and get fit. However, their prime motivation for joining is to meet new friends.

The health club markets its business by promoting the range of fitness machines, qualified instructors and superb swimming pool. However, what the new member really wants is to mix with new people. This is sometimes known as the DBM or dominant buying motive.

When marketing and selling your business you need to consider the emotional and hidden benefits of your product or service, and communicate them to the potential customer. The customer can then make a decision based on their DBM.

Business buyers are also emotional

It's not only in their personal buying decisions that people are driven by their emotions; business buyers are also emotional.

A business buyer might tell you that he wants to buy a product or service that saves his organization money. However, he might be buying it to make him look good in front of his boss – another emotional decision.

Warren Buffett, the Chairman of Berkshire Hathaway, and one of the world's richest men once remarked: 'I have walked away from some very good deals because I didn't *like* the people involved' – another emotional decision.

It doesn't matter if your product or service is predominantly technical or something much simpler; the person who buys it will always be driven by their emotions, so you ignore that at your peril.

It's difficult to be logical

It's often extremely difficult for a customer to make a logical decision about a product or service. Most people aren't qualified to tell a good accountant from a bad one, a good lawyer from a not so good one, one washing machine from another, or one builder or plumber from another. Customers will often make a decision based on how they feel about the person they're dealing with.

A friend who was opening a new coffee shop business was telling me about her lawyer. 'Is he any good?' I asked. She replied, 'He's great; he's really nice and he doesn't talk like a lawyer!'

If my friend feels that way about her lawyer, then it'll be so much easier for both of them to do business and she'll be less concerned about how much he bills her for.

Knowing what people really want

People want certain things when they spend their own or their company's money. As stated above, they'll move towards pleasure and away from pain. For pleasure they want the following.

- **More money**. So show them how to get it, or how to save it.

- **To be liked**. Customers will spend their money with people who like them and whom they like.

- **To have fun**. Southwest Airlines in the US market flying with them as *fun*. Some other airlines market flying with them as *safe*. Most passengers take safe as a given – give your customers some fun.

- **To live longer**. Don't market healthy foodstuffs or lifestyle – instead market a longer life.

- **To be happy**. Doesn't everyone?

- **To be healthy**. Show customers how what you do minimizes stress and contributes to their good health.

- **To be respected**. Meet that need for people and you'll have a customer for life.

- **To be smarter**. Think about how your product or service can meet that need.

- **To have peace of mind**. If customers buy from you, will they sleep easier in their bed?

- **To be praised**. A very basic need for people – so do it, it won't hurt.

KNOWING WHAT THEY DON'T WANT

People are often motivated to buy in order to avoid pain. It may be the opposite of what's above but consider what we all want to avoid.

- **Losing money**. It's why people buy financial services and anything else that stops them losing their cash.

- **Rejection**. This is probably a human being's biggest fear so that's why they'll go to great lengths to avoid it.

- **Failure**. Show them how your product or service helps them avoid it.

- **Criticism**. People don't want criticism from others. That's one of the reasons we buy brands which we know others will accept.

- **Looking foolish**. Be aware of this, if you're asking someone to take a risk when buying your product or service.

- **Death**. If you've got a product or service that postpones it for a while, then I'll have some too.

UNDERSTANDING WHAT PEOPLE *REALLY* BUY

We are going to look at how we use features and benefits when it comes to making a sales presentation to a customer. But for the moment, I just want you to be really clear about what your customers want from your product or service.

Features are the characteristics of your product or service; what it has or what it does. Benefits are what those characteristics do for the customer.

As you've seen from the lists above, people don't buy what things do – they buy results.

The features of a bed that you might be selling could include 'Unique interlinked springs with a triangular structure and up to seven times as many as other beds.' (I took this statement from a bed manufacturer's website.) However, the benefit that the customer really wants is 'A good night's sleep, free from back pain.' This is what is sometimes known as the DBM. I don't promote sales training seminars to my clients, instead I promote 'More sales and an increase in profits.'

When people consider your product or service they're only thinking one thing: 'What's in it for me?' Any communication with your customers has to answer that question.

Have a look at some product brochures and business websites, including your own. As you read, identify the number of times you see the words 'we' or 'our' starting a sentence.

For example, 'Our company has been established for 50 years. We have a quality of service second to none. Our product contains the best of ingredients which meet all safety standards.'

If you change the words 'we' to 'you' and 'our' to 'your' at the start of the sentence, you get something like – 'You will benefit from our 50 years of experience. Your tummy will love our superb ingredients.'

If you are to become a successful businessperson, and draw customers to you, then you must remember:

> Customers do not buy products they only buy *benefits* and *solutions* to their problems; they buy good feelings.

SOME POINTS TO REMEMBER

- **Don't rely on logic.** Many people who sell a *technical* product or service often find this hard to understand. They seem to believe that all the customer is interested in is all the facts and figures. Perhaps they are, but what happens if they don't particularly like the salesperson?

- **People sell to people.** Before accepting what you say, people need to *buy* you first. If you find this hard to accept, think about people who have tried to sell you something, including a politician or a religious leader on television. If you don't particularly *like* the person then you'll find it so much harder to accept what they're saying.

- **People like people who are just like themselves**. It's important to build rapport, to establish mutual areas of interest, to show you understand and care about the other person's needs.

- **People are different**. Everyone on earth is different; we are all as different as our fingerprints. You may have similar interests, but aspects of your product or service may not be as important to your customer or client as you believe.

- **Don't stereotype**. Always keep an open mind when dealing with the other person. They may not think or behave as you'd expect.

- **Adapt your behaviour to different people**. Learn to *mirror* the other person's words, tone of voice and body language. This doesn't mean mimicking the other person; it's about communicating with them in their style and language. For example, if your customer spoke quietly and slowly, then it would build rapport if you spoke quietly and slowly, too. Subconsciously, the customer is getting the message that you are just like them.

'Turn a stranger into a friend and a friend into a customer.'
(Seth Godin)

A NEW TYPE OF SALESPERSON

In the past 20 years there has been dramatic change in the sales environment and the way customers do business. Markets around the world have become more competitive and customers need to make better buying decisions.

Most sales and businesspeople are finding that their customers are more knowledgeable, more analytical and more demanding. Salespeople find themselves selling solutions instead of just products. They need to sell to a wider and higher level group of decision makers and become (in the customer's eyes) more of a business consultant and adviser. Sadly, however, some sales-people are still living in the past, and these are the people who have given others a negative viewpoint about sales and sales-people.

UNDERSTANDING OLD STYLE SELLING

In a selling situation the old style salesperson spends time as follows.

- Approximately 5% of the sales process involves *building rapport* with the customer and getting to know him or her. It would probably amount to some small talk, such as saying hello, and talking about the weather. The objectives are just to get down to making the sale as soon as possible.

- Approximately 15% of the sale would be spent finding out about the customer and what the salesperson could sell them. It would be an attempt to *identify needs* that the customer has, such as 'What kind of car are you looking for?', 'Is there a particular mobile phone you are interested in?' or 'How many kafuffle valves are you looking for?' Quite often the sales-person is hardly listening to the answer, as they have already made up their mind what they are going to sell the customer.

- The next 50% is where the sales person really gets into their stride. This is the *presentation* or the pitch. The salesperson tells the customer all about their wonderful product or service, including all of its features and sometimes its benefits. They seem to work on the assumption that the more information they throw at the customer, the more interested in buying they will become.

- The last 30% of the sale is called the *close*. This is where the salesperson tries in whatever way they can to get the customer to buy. Salespeople are taught all sorts of closing techniques to get the customer to commit. There are many closing techniques, some of which border on manipulation or coercion.

Happily, times have changed and many salespeople realize the value of new style selling.

DISCOVERING NEW STYLE SELLING

This is almost a reverse of old style selling.

- Building *rapport* and trust with the customer will account for 40% of the sale. If the customer doesn't trust you or have good rapport with you, then there is no way they're going to believe or accept what you say.

- About 30% of the sale needs to be spent on *identifying needs*. You need to find out what the real needs of the customer are, not what you think they need. It is absolutely vital to understand the customer and their business.

- Spend about 20% of your time on *presenting* solutions to satisfy the customer's real needs. Talk about the benefits of your product or service that are relevant to the customer's needs.

■ It is still important to *close the sale* and ask for an order or some other form of commitment. However, this will only involve 10% of the sale, and it will be so much easier if the previous three steps have been completed effectively.

The modern businessperson realizes that a different approach to a selling strategy must take place in order to build business and generate the competitive edge.

SELLING IS ABOUT CHANGE

The process of selling often involves change. Your potential customer or client will most likely have an existing supplier – or a different way of doing whatever it is your product or service does. So, what kind of changes are we talking about? Changes could include:

■ a change of supplier;

■ a change of technology;

■ a change of price;

■ a change of attitude.

Most people are resistant to change. They see it as a threat rather than an opportunity. Your job is to instigate change, so you need to make the idea of change appear to be:

■ highly beneficial to the customer;

■ easy;

■ straightforward.

Sales- and businesspeople need many skills, qualities and characteristics to bring about this change. The most fundamental quality is *attitude*.

> *Our attitude toward life determines life's attitude towards us.*
> (Earl Nightingale)

2

Getting into the Mindset

The single most important characteristic that distinguishes the successful businessperson from the rest is *attitude*. Being in the right frame of mind will determine success in making a sale.

However, this can be a challenge particularly in difficult trading times. Business is much more competitive, and it's easy to become demotivated. It is also a challenge to remain positive when you lose customers or they fail to use more of your products or services. It is easy to become downhearted when a potential customer is unwilling to accept what you're proposing.

That's why you must take charge of your own physical and emotional well-being. You cannot rely on anyone else to motivate you; you have the power to do it yourself.

'Ability is what you're capable of doing. Motivation determines what you do. Attitude determines how well you do it.'

(Lou Holtz)

FIVE STEPS TO SUCCESS

1. Thinking

How you think and your relationship with yourself, is what will decide how well you communicate with everyone connected to your business. And that will decide your success. The most important relationship you will ever have is the one you have with yourself, so you must get that right. How you think will control your emotions and resultantly how you act. Too often we *react* to our inbuilt programmes and don't think. The successful business person does not react – they think.

Why do we react most of the time?

First of all, we need to understand ourselves better and consider why we behave as we do. Man is an amazingly complex and complicated animal. Years of study, research and experimentation haven't yet answered all the questions about the human mind.

The mind is often compared to an iceberg, with the conscious mind being the 10% above the waterline and the subconscious the 90% that is submerged.

The conscious mind deals with all the intellectual left-brain thinking activities. The subconscious mind handles the right-brain activities, plus all the day-to-day automatic functions such as:

- heartbeat;
- blood pressure;
- temperature control;
- breathing;
- chemical balance;
- digestive process.

Our subconscious records everything that has ever been programmed in through our five senses. It stores our memories and experiences and our feelings, beliefs, attitudes, habits and perceptions.

The subconscious has an almost unlimited capacity for storing and processing information. Some experts believe it stores everything we've ever seen, heard or experienced.

The subconscious mind, which is the source of all your power, will always dominate your conscious mind. If an idea has been programmed in, it's very difficult to change it. You'll have experienced people with beliefs which you may want to change, but you find this almost impossible to do.

When it comes to you, however, the situation is different. It's *your* mind, and you have the power to change it.

Experiments show that the conscious mind can program the subconscious. This can have an effect on:

■ physical health;

■ athletic performance;

■ mental ability;

■ motivation.

Much of the time your subconscious works against you, because many of its programs are incorrect. People who were told when they were young that they were ugly or stupid, or would never amount to anything, still run these negative programs.

When faced with any situation, your subconscious will try to deal with it, and you react. As I've said, successful people don't react, they think, so you need to operate from your conscious mind and *think*.

Using positive self-talk

Let me tell you a story. When I was working in the beer industry I was intrigued by our top ten successful bar- and hotel-owning customers. The majority of them, to put it tactfully, didn't seem to be particularly sophisticated businesspeople. In other words, they didn't seem to have had any kind of business training or any qualifications.

I was discussing with my boss one day how these people had become so successful and he said, 'They don't know they can't do it. You and I, Alan, see the pitfalls, we know about business and we see all the ways we could fail. These people only think about how they'll succeed.'

As you'll gather, this was a pretty powerful message for me – these successful business owners were *talking to themselves* in a much more positive way than less successful people.

Your level of success in terms of your happiness, emotional well-being and anything else you desire is a direct result of how you think and how you talk to yourself.

Listen to the self-talk that goes on in your head and ask yourself 'Is what I'm saying allowing me to be confident, on top and going for it?' If so – great! 'Or is it holding me back and stopping me achieving my goals?' If this is the case – *stop it*, change the program.

By talking to yourself in a positive manner, you'll start to feel physically better. Words have an enormous power to change the chemistry of your body. Your heart rate, blood pressure, muscles, nerves and breathing will all react to the words you say to yourself.

Take a moment to say some words to yourself such as 'holidays', 'warm sunshine', 'sandy beaches', 'swimming', 'chilled beer', 'delicious food'. Are you starting to get good feelings? I hope you are. Maybe words like 'home', 'family', 'children', or 'Christmas' give you some good feelings. Or how about the word 'sex'? I bet that could change the chemistry of your body.

So think about the things you say to yourself and make every statement in the present tense.

Don't say, for example, 'I'm going to make a success of this business' or 'I'm going to get organized,' or 'I'm going to be much more confident.'

Instead say, 'I am totally in control of my life and my business. I am totally confident and positive. I'm achieving my goals. I have determination and drive.'

What you're doing here is reprogramming your subconscious. If you talk to yourself in a positive way, that's what your subconscious will focus on.

Top sportspeople know all about self-talk; they know that they need to talk to themselves in a positive way to be successful. Research has proved that the success of the world's top golfers is determined by 20% physical ability and 80% mental ability. In the day-to-day tasks that we face in our life, we should be no different from sportspeople.

If you talk to yourself in a negative way that's what your subconscious will focus on. If you think illness, you'll become ill. If you think doom and gloom, that's what you'll get. But if you think 'health, happiness and success', you're already there.

In the city where I live, parking a car can be difficult. Say, for example, I need to visit a bookstore and I decide to take my car. I say to myself 'I'm going to park my car outside the bookstore.'

If I have someone with me they'll inevitably say, 'You're nuts Alan, you'll never get parked there, far better to park several blocks away in a quieter area.' And guess what – most of the time I park outside the bookstore, or very close to it. It doesn't happen all the time, but talking to yourself in a positive way is much more likely to get you the results you want.

You have the power to reprogram your mind, replace your old conditioning, and get more out of life. You do this by thinking and using positive self-talk.

Put this to the test right away; for the next seven days listen to what you say to yourself and if it's negative, change it to something more positive and you'll start to feel better, look better and have much more success.

> *'Every waking moment we talk to ourselves about the things we experience. Our self-talk, the thoughts we communicate to ourselves, in turn control the way we feel and act.'*
>
> (John Lembo)

2. Believing

No one is going to believe in you until you believe in yourself. Your belief in yourself is so apparent by the way you talk, walk and conduct yourself.

Not many people are drawn to a person who is so overflowing with self-belief that it makes them impossible to deal with. However, you still need to constantly work on your self-belief.

■ Concentrate on what you do well, not what you don't.

■ Concentrate on what you've done, not what you haven't achieved.

■ Concentrate on what you do, not what you don't.

Overcoming negative programming

Some people are fortunate to have been brought up in an environment that develops their self-belief. Their parents and their upbringing encouraged them to be as good as they can be.

I was listening to a colleague talking on the phone to her six-year-old child the other day. He was telling her about his school sports day and how well he had done in the race he'd entered. I heard Penny say, 'Well done, fantastic, that's great, I'm really proud of you!' It turned out that her little boy had come second in his race, and it made me think how some other parents might react. They might have said, 'Too bad you didn't win. That's a pity. Never mind, better luck next time. Who was it who came first in the race?'

Which of these responses is going to develop a child's belief in himself? Obviously it is the first reaction. If Penny's little boy receives that kind of response for being second what does he think he will receive for being first? The second response only reduces the child's belief in himself.

Sadly, the majority of us do not receive regular boosts to our self-belief. But that doesn't mean we can't change it.

> *'What the mind of man can conceive and believe, it can achieve.'*
> (Napoleon Hill)

Take a moment, find a piece of paper and write down all the things you have achieved in your life. Don't trivialize anything, write it down. We often think that some of the things we've achieved are not such a big deal. I know people with a university degree who don't think it's that important. Well, I don't have one and I wish I did. But I don't let it bother me; I just think about the fact that I've written two best selling books and I'm now writing this third one.

Think about your superpowers, all the qualities you have, the things you are good at. How do you rate in:

- determination;

- popularity;

- dignity;

- humour;

- sex appeal;

- calm disposition;

- approachability;

- generosity?

Are you intelligent?

I am always intrigued by people who are described as 'intelligent.' What does this mean and why is it so valued? That's why I was so interested in the studies of Howard Gardner, a psychologist at Harvard University. Gardner's theory of multiple intelligences states that not only do human beings have many different ways to learn and process information, but that these are independent of each other; leading to multiple *intelligences* as opposed to a general intelligence among correlated abilities. In 1999 Gardner listed seven intelligences.

1. **Linguistic intelligence.** This concerns language and how we use it. Writers, poets, lawyers and speakers are among those who Howard Gardner sees as having high linguistic intelligence.

2. **Logical–mathematical intelligence.** This is associated with calculation and logical reasoning. This intelligence is most often linked to scientific and mathematical thinking.

3. **Musical intelligence.** To do with musical appreciation as well as performing and composing music.

4. **Bodily–kinaesthetic intelligence.** Associated with physical skills like sport, dancing and other aspects of movement.

5. **Spatial intelligence.** To do with art and design, as well as finding your way around.

6. **Interpersonal intelligence.** To do with interacting with people socially and sensitively. It's concerned with the capacity to understand the intentions, motivations and desires of other people. Educators, salespeople, religious and political leaders and counsellors all need a well-developed interpersonal intelligence.

7. **Intrapersonal intelligence.** Concerned with understanding yourself, to appreciate your feelings, fears, motivations and abilities.

So the next time someone tells you about a so-called *intelligent* person, ask what they know about design, or the ability to deal with other people, or what musical instrument they play.

Always remember that you have qualities and skills that other people do not have and you should be proud of these and *believe* in yourself. When you look at this list, you may realise that you are much more intelligent than you think.

> 'There is no such thing as Intelligence; one has intelligence of this or that. One must have intelligence only for what one is doing.'
>
> (Edgar Degas)

Another tip for self-motivation

I have a confession to make: on occasion I have felt a little demotivated. Yes, me, the 'Motivation Doctor', feels a bit lacking in motivation and self-belief from time to time, just like everybody else.

So, here is something that works for me – *spend time with positive people.*

Most Saturdays I have lunch with five of my really good friends. They're always interested in what I'm doing, are really supportive and they make me laugh! When I leave them, I feel much better and more motivated than I did before we met.

I like to think that I do the same for them, and that's the secret to receiving support and motivation from others; you need to hand out some *warm glows.* Help other people feel better about themselves, build their self-belief and that in turn will build your belief in yourself.

I remember reading in the newspapers some years ago that Richard Branson, the entrepreneur, was going to start an airline. I knew he had been successful in other areas of business, but starting an airline seemed a mammoth task to me. He was going into competition with the world's largest airlines that had been in the business for years. I didn't believe he had a chance. However, Richard leased his first aeroplane, started Virgin Atlantic and as you know, the rest is history.

Step out of your comfort zone

Sir Richard Branson is not a particularly well educated person in terms of academic qualifications. However, he has belief in himself and what he's doing, and that is one of the qualities that drives him forward.

So, step out of your comfort zone, take risks, and believe in yourself.

3. Energising yourself

Your success in making more sales is highly dependent on your levels of energy. You need energy in your brain and you need energy in your body. However, just like any other form of energy, it is constantly being consumed and your batteries need recharging.

Dealing with people, your customers, your suppliers, your bank manager, and all the people in your personal life drains your brain and your body. So you need to hold onto as much energy as you can, and generate more.

Conserving brain energy

Imagine that you have just received a letter from your bank manager saying something like 'Please make an appointment to meet me and discuss your account.' If you react to that with 'Oh no! What does he want, what's wrong now? Maybe he wants to recall my loan.' That sort of reaction will drain your brain energy and give you stress.

Remember what I said above? The successful businessperson does not react – they think. *Reacting drains the brain – thinking, less so.*

Get the thinking bit working and say to yourself: 'I'll phone him now; I'll speak to him and see what he wants. If it's about the poor business results, what information do I need to make my case? Perhaps he wants to talk about how I could develop the business.'

Whatever you're thinking – stop the negative stuff – it'll kill you!

If someone comes to you with a problem, or you receive a customer complaint, or an unexpected demand from the tax man; start thinking 'Let's see what I can do about this.'

My favourite thinking words are 'Deal with it!' Whatever happens, that's what I say to myself.

It's also important to avoid other external influences that will drain your brain. We are surrounded by a great deal of negativity. Newspapers and TV news thrives on negative stories, not positive ones. I suggest that you're very selective about the news that you watch or read about. It's important to keep up with what is happening in the world, but an overload of negative energy will drain your brain and seriously inhibit your success.

There is a TV soap opera on British TV called *EastEnders*, it's been running for years and has a huge following. Every time I've ever watched part of it, (that's all I could stand), all I've ever seen is people crying, fighting, arguing and involved in some other negative drama.

Watching this programme will not make you feel uplifted, positive, and eager to get out and make a success of your business and your life. It will drain your brain energy.

Switch off the TV and read a book that inspires you. Learn about how other successful people run their business and their life. Do things that exercise your brain, build up the energy and the thinking muscles.

Of course it's OK to watch TV, but don't just switch it on and see what's there. Check your TV guide and decide what programmes you want to watch. Avoid all the depressing stuff. Choose programmes that inspire you, educate you and make you laugh.

Boosting body energy

Every January and February the gym I attend is crammed with new members all fulfilling their New Year resolution to get fit or lose weight. By March or April many of these people have disappeared. They get bored, they don't see any measurable results, and they give up and go back to slumping in front of the TV every night.

The successful businessperson does not give up.

> 'Never give in, never give in, never; never; never; never – in nothing, great or small, large or petty – never give in except to convictions of honour and good sense.'
>
> (Winston Churchill)

You don't have to become a gym bunny or run marathons every weekend, but you do need a good level of physical fitness if you want to be successful in making sales.

If you are a member of a gym, think about getting a personal trainer to motivate you, or even do some fitness classes. I've been doing fitness classes for years. It disciplines me to turn up at the appointed time, and I feel motivated being surrounded by like-minded individuals. I also enjoy the social chats with the friends I've made in the classes.

If that's not your thing, then there are other activities that could push up your heart rate, increase your breathing and make you sweat a little.

I spent time recently using a friend's Wii sports pack video console. I didn't realise that standing in front of a TV, playing golf, cycling, or any of the other sports programmes, could be so much fun, push up the heart rate and increase my breathing.

There are so many things you can do to boost your energy: learn to dance, make love, have a laugh, go swimming, and mix with positive friends.

Avoid the lift and the escalator, take the stairs and run up them if you can. If I take the escalator, I always walk up it and walk down it. Walk quickly when you walk because it's good for you physically and mentally. And forget about sauntering down the street with your earphones plugged in, listening to music. Become more aware of what's around you; use your eyes, your ears and your sense of smell. Observe people, read advertising, listen to what people are saying and listen to what's going on around you – *get into the world.*

Look after your body and your brain and it will help you *make that sale.*

4. Relating to others

It makes sense to say that successful sales- and businesspeople are good at relating to others; they are good at building rapport. Some people are naturally good at relating to people, while others just have to work that little bit harder.

Relating to other people is not just about talking to them; it's about listening and building a bond with everyone you meet. You'll note I say 'everyone', and I mean everyone. If you are in business and you want to sell your product or service, then you need to regard everyone as a potential customer or someone who could influence a potential customer. The person beside you in the gym changing room, the parents of your children's friends, and everyone you come into contact with, could be a potential customer.

I used to pass the time of day with my next door neighbour Dave, whenever we met in the car park of our apartment block. I thought Dave was an engineer with a telecommunications company, and didn't believe he offered me any business opportunities. However, we used to chat and I made sure that he knew what my business was all about. One day when we met, he asked me if I would be able to do some customer service training at his company. It turned out that he was a senior manager and he wanted his engineers to have better skills when dealing with customers. That provided me with a great deal of work with his telecommunications company and also led me to further work within that industry.

And forget what your mother said about not talking to strangers – always talk to strangers!

Warm glows

Let me ask you – do you remember how you felt after your last interaction with another person, either on the phone or face to face? That person could have been one of your customers, a colleague, a salesperson, a friend or a member of your family. Did they make you feel good, uplifted and more positive? Did they leave you feeling neutral or, even worse, did they make you feel down and more negative?

It is so easy to make negative comments to other people. We say things like, 'The weather is really bad today', 'What do you think about that murder that was reported in the news this morning?' or 'Did you see that report about the downturn in the economy?'

If customers leave an interaction with you feeling better than they did before, then they're much more likely to deal with you again, recommend you to other people and spend more money with you. If any other person feels better after an interaction with you, then they're much more likely to pass that feeling on to someone else. If a friend feels better and more motivated after spending time in your company, then they're much more likely to return these feelings to you.

So, go ahead; give five positive and motivational comments to the other people in your life, in proportion to one negative comment. You'll have a more productive business, more fun, more happy customers, more friends, better relationships, and a healthier, happier and longer life. *Hand out warm glows, not dampeners.*

> *'Pretend that every single person you meet has a sign around his or her neck that says, "Make me feel important". Not only will you succeed in sales, you will succeed in life.'*
>
> (Mary Kay Ash)

5. Do it

If you want to make more sales, and I'm sure you do, then you need courage, you need to take action, and you need to *do it now*. You need to pick up that phone, make cold calls, talk to people at networking events, ask for the order, and any other action you need to take to further your business.

To do or not to do

If you're like me, you probably have a 'to-do' list of some kind or another; and if not, why not? It might be part of a sophisticated online planning system, or written in a diary or notebook, or even scribbled on the back of an envelope. However, I am now suggesting that you have a *don't-do* list, or a *stop-doing* list.

I once had an assistant who one day proudly showed me her to-do list with 54 activities on it. In the time it took her to write this list, she could have completed 75% of the activities.

If you have a huge to-do list, sit down and take a closer look at it. Ask yourself if you *really* need to do everything on that list. Perhaps you have a partner, a member of your staff, or even a member of your family who you could delegate some of these tasks to. Remember the saying 'Only do it if only you can do it'.

There may even be activities on your list – and brace yourself – that you don't really have to do at all.

Here's another question to ask yourself – 'Is what I'm doing now getting me to where I want to get to; is it helping me to achieve what I want to achieve?' If the answer is 'No', *stop doing it*.

STICKING TO THE 80/20 RULE

Remember the Pareto Principle, the 80/20 rule: 80% of your results come from 20% of your activities. This means that the activities you do for 20% of your time, need to be increased if you want to improve your results.

I once read some background material on J.K. Rowling , the highly successful Harry Potter author. When she was writing her first book, she lived in a small apartment in my home city of Edinburgh. By her own admission, she didn't spend too much time doing the domestic chores; she was much more concerned with getting her book finished and finding a publisher.

Now I'm not suggesting that you work in a dirty or untidy environment, as that can only lead to inefficiency and poor work. However, I am suggesting that you keep completely focused on your goal, target, ambition or whatever it is you want to call it. And only do what you need to do to achieve it.

> Be like a stamp – stick to it till you get to your destination.

One goal

I've been reading and listening for years to motivational speakers who tell you that you must have goals. You must write them down for all aspects of your life – your business, your family, your education, spirituality, personal development, friends and financial matters. However, I've come to the conclusion that successful people don't necessarily do all that stuff. They don't spend time working on lists and filling out plans. They take action; they *do it,* whatever it takes to achieve whatever it is they want to achieve.

Tiger Woods wanted to be the best golfer in the world. Muhammad Ali wanted to be the best boxer the world had ever seen. Sir Richard Branson wanted to build a successful business empire. I don't think they spent too much time sitting around writing lists.

A key secret of success

Successful people never give up. This is what separates the winners from the losers in business, in sport and in life. If you have a mountain to climb either literally or figuratively and you reach an obstacle – don't quit. Find another way round; even go back a short distance and come back at the situation from another direction. If you make a mistake, then you will learn from that situation and never do it again. Remember: *the person who never made a mistake, never made anything.*

Whatever it is you're trying to do, whatever success you want – never quit. Make mistakes, fall down, get up, fall down, but get up and try again. Never, never, never give up.

SEVEN SIMPLE STEPS TO GET MORE OUT OF YOUR DAY

Let's face it, time is probably your greatest resource. You never seem to have enough of it, and it seems to pass so quickly. Well, you won't get any more of it, and you can't slow it down.

What you can do is make the most of the time you have. Here are some simple steps you can take to get the most out of your day.

1. **Plan your day the night before**. At the end of each day write out all the things you need to do the following day to achieve

your goal. Pull together all the information you'll need, phone numbers and relevant paperwork.

2. **Prioritise the list**. Number each item and do the nasty jobs first. There's always the temptation to do the easy jobs first. However, think how the thought of doing the nasty jobs hangs over you as you do the easy stuff. Think how good you'll feel when the nasties are out of the way, and how motivated you'll feel.

3. **Stick to your list**. Tick off each item as you go, and don't let yourself be distracted. The temptation is to handle the telephone and e-mails as they come in. The phone is hard to ignore but you could always pull out the plug and let it go to voice mail and switch off the e-mail program. Make an agreement with yourself to check for messages every two hours or so.

4. **Remember the Three Ds**. Do it, Delegate it or Dump it. Handle each piece of paper only once. Either do something about it now, delegate it to someone else, or throw it in the waste bin. And remember – *only do it if only you can do it.*

5. **Don't procrastinate**. Procrastination really is the *Thief of Time*. It's so easy to put things off till another time or until, 'I've had time to think about it.' Don't put it off – *do it now.*

6. **Plan your leisure time**. Take up activities that need you to be at a certain place at a certain time. Instead of just going to the gym, book a fitness class or an appointment with a personal trainer.

7. **Be honest with yourself**. Remember what I said above. Keep asking, 'Is what I'm doing now getting me to where I want to get to?' If the answer is 'no', then *change what you're doing*.

> This is the easiest way to get more out of your day and more out of your life. And, to use the Nike slogan, 'Just do it!'

3

Motivating People to Buy

It almost goes without saying that you need to be proactive and approach potential customers to sell your product or service, and we're going to look at that in Chapter 5. But there is so much more you could be doing to get those potential customers to come to you, and keep coming back. *You motivate them to buy.*

MOMENTS OF TRUTH

'How do you find new customers or clients for your business?' It's a question I often ask businesspeople, usually because I'm hoping to learn something new. The answer that comes back most often is 'Most of our customers come from word of mouth!'

So my next questions is 'So what do you do to generate more word of mouth?' I never really get an answer to that one.

There are many things you can do to generate word of mouth and I call them 'moments of truth'.

Some years ago, I was running seminars for managers and customer service people from a UK bank. I was having a chat one day with the manager of the hotel where the seminars were taking place. We were discussing the participants on the course and he said, 'These people are really nice, they are so easy to deal with.'

Do you think that this manager is a potential customer for the bank? You bet he is! And could also have a positive influence on other people that he knows? Of course he could. This is a 'moment of truth' for the bank.

People talk to each other about where they spend or invest their money. Sadly, customers are more likely to tell others about a bad experience than a good one. However, they do talk about good service in a positive way about the organizations they deal with. What would they say about yours?

Recently, I was running seminars for a software company. I was booked by the general manager; however, I remember meeting the sales manager on several occasions. He was curt, unfriendly and somewhat dismissive. Maybe he had no reason to be friendly with me; after all, I'm unlikely to be a potential customer. However, I do move in business circles, and I even know some of his potential customers. I'll let you work out the rest, another 'moment of truth'.

Every day of your life you are selling yourself. Someone you or your colleagues talk to today could be a future customer for your business. If not, then they might know someone who could be.

It is vital to generate positive 'moments of truth' every day; so how do you do it?

PROVIDING ORDINARY OR EXTRAORDINARY SERVICE

The most important way to generate positive 'moments of truth', is to provide *extraordinary customer service*. Ordinary customer service just won't do it. And of course, the difference between ordinary and extraordinary is just that little bit *extra*. Let me give you an example. I recently returned from one of my regular trips to Asia where I was conducting management seminars. While there, I also enjoyed some well earned rest and recuperation. I used three hotels, two airlines, several restaurants, and all the other services that a businessperson or tourist might use.

Aircraft departed on time, hotels provided the services detailed in their brochure, and restaurants served up some delicious meals; all things that I would describe as ordinary customer service. However, none of this would necessarily make me loyal to these businesses or recommend them to other people – it takes more.

One night in Singapore found me wandering around Little India looking for the restaurant that could serve the perfect curry. After much searching I decided on one particular place – must have been the sign outside – 'We serve the perfect curry!' The food was good and the service was fast and efficient, but no more so than any other restaurants I'd used in the past.

What made the difference for me was one small incident. After taking my food order, the manager returned to my table and introduced himself. He respectfully asked what had brought me to Singapore, and showed great interest in what I had to say. He was warm, friendly and told me how proud he was to be Singaporean. He then shook my hand, wished me success and told me how pleased he'd be to see me again.

All this only took a few minutes but it made me feel really important and I felt good. Would I go back to this restaurant, of course I would; would I recommend it to other people, of course I would.

This small incident moved the service from ordinary to extraordinary. It was more than just supplying a quality product fast and efficiently. It was about introducing the human touch.

When I ask participants on my seminars for examples of extraordinary customer service, they respond with all sorts of great stories. They say things like, 'The lady I dealt with was really warm and friendly' or 'The guy in the store made me feel really important' or 'They always remember my name when I go back to that shop'. These are all human-level responses.

We tend to base our judgement of extraordinary customer service on how we're treated as humans.

Very rarely do I hear 'The goods were delivered on time' or 'They replaced my faulty items without a quibble.' We tend to take these business level responses as a given. It's the human-level responses that influence us to use the service again or recommend it to others.

When dealing with other people in any aspect of your life it's important to open the conversation on a human level before doing the business. It can be as simple as saying 'Good morning, isn't it a lovely day!' Then say something during the interaction that is not about the business at hand. When the business is complete, close the conversation on a human level. This is not about chatting incessantly about your personal life; it's about being warm, friendly and human.

Even when writing an e-mail open the message with a 'How was your weekend?' question. Deliver your business message and close on a human note.

Some people nowadays will tell you that there's no time for human-level responses, and that customers want you to cut straight to the business. However a short human-level response can speed up the business and make your life so much easier.

Human beings have a massive need for acknowledgement from others. We want to know that other people care about us, that we're important and that we're accepted. If we satisfy that need in others by communicating on a human level as well as a business level, then all our interactions will be much more productive.

What customers really want can be divided into two areas. Firstly, they want your product or service to meet their needs and represent value for money – the *business level*; this is vital. However, even when your product or service meets the needs and expectations of your customers, it doesn't necessarily motivate them to return and spend more money – it takes more. This is the second area, the *human level*, and the deciding factor in the success of your business.

SEVEN STEPS THAT MAKE THE DIFFERENCE

1. **Warm friendly responses**. When customers meet you face to face or speak to you on the telephone, they want to feel that you're pleased to see them and happy to help. For example, it's not so important what you say when you answer the telephone, but more important how you say it.

2. **Make them feel important.** They understand that you have lots of other customers and clients. But they just love it when you make them feel special.

3. **Listen to them.** Listening is probably the most important skill

to develop when dealing with people. It's been said that people are either speaking or waiting to speak. In order to build rapport with customers it's important to listen and show that you're listening. People like good listeners; listening gives you information and indicates to the other person that you're interested in them and value what they say.

4. **Use names.** A person's name is very important to them, and you get it wrong at your peril. Make sure you say it properly, and ensure that you spell it correctly in any e-mail or letter. When you use a customer's name, it indicates that you recognize them as an individual. Don't use it too often as it can become irritating, but definitely include it at the start and end of a conversation.

5. **Be flexible.** It's not always possible to say 'Yes' to a customer or to do exactly what they want. People hate to hear the word 'No' or 'It can't be done.' It's important to be as flexible as you can. Tell people what you can do, not what you can't.

6. **Recover fast and well.** It is inevitable that things will go wrong from time to time. When things do go wrong, customers want you to solve their problems quickly. They will often judge the quality of your service by the way you recover. They will even forgive your mistakes if you recover well. They don't want to hear excuses or who's to blame or why it happened, they just want it fixed fast.

7. **They want to feel good**. Overall, customers just want to feel good. They want to feel better after they've dealt with you or anyone in your business, than they did before. If you can create that feeling, then you're well on the way to giving your customers extraordinary service.

This is what will motivate customers to return, spend more money with your business and tell their friends.

HOW TO LOSE MORE CUSTOMERS

Have you ever thought about why you lose customers? I read a survey recently that suggested customers leave a business for four basic reasons.

1. Dissatisfaction with the quality of the product or service accounts for 14%.

2. A further 9% leave because of price.

3. Just 5% leave for other reasons such as they die, leave the area or have no further need for your product or service.

4. And wait for it – a whacking great 72% leave because of *supplier indifference.*

Over the past few months four of my friends have cancelled their membership of the gym that I attend. They haven't given up on their fitness regime, they've just moved to other gyms that are much smaller and more personal. They just felt that the gym they were members of didn't seem to care whether they were there or not (supplier indifference). The facilities at the gym are good but the communication with the staff could be much improved.

Too many organizations give customers the impression that they don't care about repeat business. I've stayed in hotels and dealt with banks, stores and many suppliers who didn't seem to care whether I came back or not. A member of staff at one budget airline recently told me that if I didn't like being delayed for two and a half hours then I could always go elsewhere.

We need to let our customers know continually that we care about them. We need to keep in touch, write to them, send them information and occasionally phone them. And we certainly need to respond to their phone calls to us.

When they contact us we need to make sure we sound warm, friendly, pleased to hear from them, efficient, and maybe even look and sound like we're fun to do business with.

It's not a lot different from our personal relationships. If we don't keep telling the people close to us how much we care, or keep writing and phoning, then we shouldn't be surprised if they leave us one day.

Remember the saying – *'When should you tell your partner that you care about them? – Before somebody else does!'*

Use logic and emotion to keep customers. Give them the best products and service and value for money. However, always remember that your competitors will be doing much the same thing. The difference will be determined by how you communicate face to face, on the phone, by letter or e-mail.

Boosting your business image

Another way to generate 'moments of truth' and motivate people to buy, is to ensure you have a fantastic business image.

I'm sure you've heard the saying 'You never get a second chance to make a good first impression.' If you want to draw customers to your business then everything about it must make a good first impression. And that includes:

■ you;

■ your business name;

■ your business cards;

■ your staff;

■ your vehicles;

■ your stationery;

■ everything and anything else about your business.

We'll look at your image when we get to the section on networking, for the moment let's look at business names.

CONJURING UP THE BEST BUSINESS NAME

It's very important to get your business name right. You may already have a business name but it's not too late to change it. Big organizations change their business and product names all the time.

I named my business Fairweather Associates when I started in 1993. However, when I attended networking events with my name badge on my lapel, people would assume that I was from a firm of accountants, or architects, or who knows what. They would come up with everything except what I actually did, which was professional speaking, writing and consulting.

Here are some things to think about when choosing your business name.

■ Make it easy to remember. I met a lady from a graphic design business called 'Shout' – I always remembered that name.

■ Make it easy to pronounce.

- Make it easy to spell.

- Stir your customer's interest; make them want to ask more. 'Jones the Plumbers' doesn't exactly do it. I once met someone from 'Dynamic Plumbers' and I had to ask 'What makes you Dynamic?'

- Make it positive sounding and optimistic.

- Make it changeable – your company 'Apex Software' might want to start selling hardware someday.

- Make sure it doesn't confuse you with someone else.

- Make it attract the kind of customers you want. A friend of mine owns a business called Equi-store. As the name might tell you, it sells all sorts of equestrian products to the horsy set.

- Make it fun (if it's appropriate for your business). For example, 'Curl up and Dye' for a hairdresser.

- Make it quirky, such as egg.com. Would you believe it's a bank?

Here are some suggestions to help you choose a name.

- Brainstorm. Think about how you want people to feel when they see or hear your name. Touch the emotions.

- Think of humorous aspects of what you do.

- Check other names and trademarks on the internet.

- Check domain names.

- Does your name sound cheap or expensive?

■ Think about picking a name that starts with an 'A'. That could be important if you want to be listed in a publication such as *Yellow Pages*.

■ Ask people who don't know your business what your business name means to them.

CREATING BUSINESS CARDS THAT DO THE BUSINESS

A business card makes a statement about who you are and what your business is about. It needs to convey the quality of your business and an insight into your personality.

I have been handed business cards and the first thought to go through my mind was 'Cheap!' A tacky design printed on low quality paper doesn't feel good in the hand and looks cheap. That then becomes my overall impression of the business. Here are some ideas.

■ Find a designer, a professional you can work with and trust. It doesn't have to be expensive, and will add so much value to your business.

■ Have a clear idea in your mind what you are looking for, discuss it with the designer, make suggestions, and trust them.

■ Use colour. Black and white is too boring but don't use 'day-glo' colours because they look cheap.

■ Include your photograph – it will help people remember you and make that important human contact. The photograph needs to face into the text, not away from it and be of good quality. It should not be a 'mugshot'.

- Use quality paper. My business cards are made from a really durable card that doesn't get dog-eared easily and are difficult to tear up.

- Add your logo. Make the logo small, you've a lot more important information to put on your card. You don't necessarily need a logo but it helps give you an identity.

- Make it a standard shape. However you can use a fold-over which gives more space for text and looks different. I used to have a card like a small tent card. I've seen it several times standing on a customer's desk. It looked too good to throw away.

- Do something different. Have a card that stops people in their tracks and makes them want to find out more.

- Display benefit statements prominently on the card. Tell customers what you can do for them and how you can help solve their problems. Your name and your business details should be much less prominent.

- Use both sides of the card. If you include a photo, benefit statements and all your business details, then you'll need both sides of the card. Business details can go on one side and benefit statements on the other.

- Don't squeeze too much in – it can start to look messy.

- Contact information should include your business name, address, phone, e-mail and website. I avoid including my mobile phone number because it can always be written on for special customers. This lets them know that I only give this number to certain people.

- Your name should be shown as you'd like to be addressed when a customer calls you. You don't need to add middle initials. Also avoid including all your qualifications, the majority of people aren't impressed by all the exams you've passed. They only want to know if you can solve their problems and they could even be put off by a whole string of letters.

- The text should be easy to read. Don't use all capital letters and limit the number of typefaces. Remember that fancy fonts can look really cheap.

- Change of details. If your details change, don't score out the old information and write the new details – order new cards. Putting little stickers on with your new information is another no-no; it makes you and your business look cheap.

Remember, you don't necessarily have to go to your local print shop for business cards. I live in the UK, but my cards and all other promotional material are designed by an excellent designer in Canada and printed in Holland.

Before we finish talking about business cards let me say *Never, never, never leave home without a business card.* Don't even dig the garden, wash the car, or visit the supermarket without a business card. You'll often meet people who say 'And what do you do?' or 'It's ages since I've seen you, what sort of business are you in now?'

I was caught out recently in the steam room at the gym. Someone I don't know too well asked me 'Could you give me some details on your business, we need a speaker at our next conference.' I didn't have a card in my birthday suit but I did have one in my gym bag which I passed on later.

WRITING SUCCESSFUL BROCHURES

Nowadays, almost every business has a website, and if you don't have one, then get one quick. However, many customers still want to look at a brochure or other form of hard copy. It's important therefore that your brochure tells the customer all they need to know.

If you are the owner of a small business, then you don't need to have an expensive multi-page brochure. Perhaps you only need a one-sheet. Just a single sheet printed on both sides with the relevant information.

■ It can be handed to the customer or used for direct mailing.

■ You can send it by e-mail as a PDF document.

■ It gives the customer much more detail.

■ It confirms what you've discussed.

■ It gives your business credibility and status.

■ It can help break the ice before you meet the customer.

The elements of a successful brochure

A successful brochure must have a call to action. You must ask the customer to do something after reading your brochure or one-sheet (particularly if you use it for mailing). This could be placing an order, requesting more information, arranging an appointment or phoning you. Tell them what to do. Make them an offer they can't refuse. For example, an early-bird discount, a special price or a never to be repeated offer. It needs to have a free-phone number, a tear-off coupon or an enclosed order form.

> Remember – this is a sales document, its purpose is to get you more orders not just to fill people's heads with information.

Think about the customer. Your brochure must talk in terms of the customer's interests, not yours. (Don't let your ego run away with you.) It must explain how you could solve the customer's problems and how it could benefit their business.

Testimonials and endorsements. Include all the statements that other people have said about your product or service. They must be real statements giving the person's name and their organization.

People won't believe statements such as 'This service is second to none – Sales Director'.

Specialize. If you're targeting a particular market, your brochure needs to reassure the customer that you understand and have expertise in that market. You then need to give examples of how you've solved specific problems in that market.

Make them want to read more. The front of your brochure must have a headline that grabs the customer and encourages them to read more. It needs to include a strong benefit or a way to solve a problem.

For example, I might produce a headline for one of my brochures that says *'Customer Service Training for the Retail Industry'*. It would be far better if I went to the heart of the problem and used the headline *'How to stop customers walking out of your store and buying from one of your competitors.'*

Think about the problems that your customers face and how your product or service resolves them and then write your headline.

The most powerful words you can use in a headline are 'how to'. It immediately grabs the reader's attention if it is relevant to them. Other great words to use are 'free', 'you', 'secrets of', 'discover', 'new' and 'announcing'.

The headline needs to be:

■ believable;

■ appealing to the emotions;

■ not more than 16 words;

■ in upper and lower case letters (not all capitals);

■ in quotation marks;

■ easy to understand.

Make it easy to read. People want to gather information quickly and aren't willing to plough through lots of text so use bullet points. You want a clean uncluttered look.

Also watch out for jargon, buzz words and technical terms. Remember the selling acronym 'KISS' (keep it simple stupid).

It doesn't need to be expensive. It makes sense to use good quality paper and it's best to stick to white or cream semi-gloss or glossy stock. Your brochure needs to feel good in the customer's hands and promote a classy, quality image.

It can contain as many pages as you like but, as I mentioned earlier, why not consider a one-sheet (which has two sides).

You could have several one-sheets produced, each relevant to the market you're targeting. You could also produce individual ones for each product or service that you provide. I have searched, frustratingly, through many a brochure trying to find specific information on a product or service.

Laminate. Buy a laminator (they're not expensive) and laminate one-sheets or pages from your brochure. This makes the information look and feel much better and encourages the customer to hang onto it for longer.

Friendly. Your brochure should give the potential customer the feeling that your business is friendly and interesting to deal with. Depending on what business you're in, you might want the customer to know that you're also fun to deal with. Don't make your brochure too businesslike even though you're selling a technical product; remember you're communicating to a human being who is driven primarily by their emotions.

It makes sense to build a relationship with a graphic designer who you like and who understands what you're trying to achieve. However, if you want to have more control, there is software you can buy and internet sites where you can create your own stationery.

WINNING WEBSITES

Customers will form an opinion of your business as soon as they look at your website. Therefore the same basic rules apply that you used in the production of your brochure and your business card (grabs attention, easy to read, includes a benefit statement, friendly and makes a statement about your business). More and more potential customers will look at your website to find out about your product or service or even to place an order. Here are some further points.

- **Keep it updated**. All information, prices and technical details need to be right up to date.

- **Easy to understand**. Just like your brochure, your customers need to find what they're looking for quickly and easily.

- **Not cluttered**. Some websites try to convey too much information and people just click off. Again, remember the KISS principle (keep it simple stupid).

- **Don't be too clever**. No fancy fonts and flashing lights. People are getting tired of sites that try to be too clever. They're designed by people who want to show how clever they are and who aren't really thinking about the customer.

- **Fast loading**. Photographs and graphics can be slow to download, so be aware. If customers can't get to what they're looking for quickly enough, then they'll click off.

- **Friendly**. Your website, just like all your other marketing materials, needs to suggest to the customer that you are a warm and friendly organization to deal with.

- **Call to action**. Every page of your website needs to tell the customer what to do next: order something, phone for more information or sign up for your newsletter.

Just to summarize this section on business image:

> Everything about your business image must create a desire in a customer or client to contact you and do business. It also needs to encourage them to recommend you to other people.

HOW TO BRAND YOUR BUSINESS

Let me ask you, do you wear a T-shirt when you go to the gym? Or, if you play golf, is a polo shirt your fashion choice? What about when you go to the mall at the weekend or to the supermarket, do you like to wear your favourite sweater?

You probably have brand names on these items of clothing: Nike, Adidas, Polo or Gap. Do these organizations pay you to promote their brand? I don't think so! So why not promote your own brand?

I strongly suggest you get a brand if you don't already have one. It could be the name of your company, a logo, or a feature of your business.

I told you about starting my business in 1993 and naming it Fairweather Associates (boring). I then changed it to PowerPlan for a few years. Then in 2002 I had a personal consultation with Dottie Walters in Los Angeles. Dottie, sadly not with us any more, was the founder of Walters Speaker Services and a leading light in the world of speakers bureaus. One piece of valuable advice she gave me was, 'Alan, get yourself a moniker'. In other words, a nickname or a brand.

I recently attended a chamber of commerce networking meeting. I introduced myself to a group of people as Alan Fairweather. One man immediately said, 'Ah, The Motivation Doctor!' Now where he had heard of me or how he knew me, I never found out, partly because he couldn't remember. But he knew that I was an international speaker and author and that pleased me no end. But I don't think he would have remembered 'Fairweather Associates'.

IT'S THE REAL THING

On 8 May 1886, a pharmacist named Dr John Pemberton carried a jug of Coca-Cola syrup to Jacobs' Pharmacy in downtown Atlanta, where it was mixed with carbonated water and sold for five cents a glass. During the first year, sales averaged a modest nine drinks per day. Dr Pemberton never realised the potential of the beverage he created. He gradually sold portions of his business to various partners and, just prior to his death in 1888, sold his remaining interest in Coca-Cola to Asa G. Candler.

A firm believer in advertising, Mr Candler expanded on Dr Pemberton's marketing efforts, distributing thousands of coupons for a complimentary glass of Coca-Cola. He promoted the product incessantly, distributing souvenir fans, calendars, clocks, urns and countless novelties, all depicting the trademark. And as they say, the rest is history.

You might not wish to have a business as big as Coca-Cola, or Nike or Google. But that should not stop you always promoting your brand.

This chapter is about motivating people to buy, and they are much more likely to buy if your business name, your brand, triggers something in their mind.

If I tried to sell you a pair of running shoes and offered you Nike or Apex shoes, which ones would you choose? I'd explain that both brands of shoes are the same quality with the exact same features. In fact, the Apex shoes are a good bit cheaper and will do the same job. The majority of people will, given this choice, choose Nike. Why? Because they are familiar with the brand, they trust the product, and they don't want to be seen at the gym wearing shoes that nobody has heard of. Remember what I said in Chapter 1 about people making emotional decisions before logical ones.

When I go to the gym, I always wear a T-shirt decorated with a picture of my latest book or my logo. And believe me I've sold quite a few books that way.

Put your brand on everything you can: your e-mail signature, website, business cards, T-shirts, baseball caps and promotional giveaways. You don't have to spend a great deal of money; just get your brand out there at every opportunity.

ONLINE NETWORKING

Online networking is another way to get your brand out there, create interest and motivate people to buy.

Are you on Twitter, Facebook, LinkedIn, YouTube, or any other networking site, and if not, why not? Many people still regard Twitter as a waste of time. They think Facebook is for teenagers, or people looking to find the love of their life. And they are not even sure what LinkedIn is all about.

I strongly suggest that you become part of the online networking community, no matter what business you are in. It's free, it doesn't have to take up much of your time, and it gets your name out there.

Sign up with Ping.fm, it's free and you can post a message that will be sent to all the networking sites you choose. You can tell the world about a new product or service, or an article you've written. You can post photos and videos, or information on your newsletter or blog. Tell the world about what you are doing, but don't be boring, make it something they will want to read and remember – get your brand in front of your online contacts.

Use YouTube to tell the world about you, your business and how you can make a difference. You can record video with most compact cameras nowadays, and your mobile phone.

However, don't just post business items. I really get annoyed by people blatantly trying to sell me their product or service on Facebook. I just delete them from my list.

Tell people something about yourself, write something human. For example, 'Just had a great weekend waterskiing, never tried it before, it was fun!' Then perhaps the next day you might post, 'Just signed a contract with a new customer for my cleaning services; they were really impressed with what we can do.'

Tell people how clever you are, what a great product or service you have, but be subtle about it.

FACE-TO-FACE NETWORKING

What is networking?

Networking is probably the oldest, easiest, most effective and least expensive way to get business to come to you. It doesn't necessarily involve selling your product or service, but it does mean selling yourself. However, that doesn't involve a lot of talking – it *does* involve a lot of listening.

Networking is about making connections with people and building a network of meaningful relationships. Having good relationships means that these people will either do business with you or recommend you to others. These people are your unpaid salesforce and you must ensure they do a good job.

Why do it?

Many businesspeople tell me that they get most of their new customers from word of mouth. When I ask them what they do to generate word of mouth business, they usually say, 'We don't do anything, it just happens.'

Just think how much more word-of-mouth business they could generate if they did something to promote it – that's where networking comes in. Networking is one of the most important things you can do to get customers to come to you.

You might have the type of business whereby potential customers check *Yellow Pages* or some other listing, or even respond to your advertising. However, as I'm sure you're aware, many people ask others when they're looking for a particular product or service.

- 'Which computer do you use, do you like it, where did you get it?'

- 'Do you know of a graphic designer I could use?'

- 'Who does your printing – what are they like to deal with?'

People talk all the time and they're more likely to do business with someone they've met and been impressed with, or have heard about from a friend or colleague.

When and where to network

You do it all the time and everywhere you go.

'I look upon every day to be lost in which I do not make a new acquaintance.'

(Samuel Johnson)

Networking can be done formally or informally. Formal networking takes place when you allocate time in your diary to get out and do it at:

■ chamber of commerce meetings;

■ networking clubs;

■ professional associations;

■ breakfast meetings;

■ Rotary clubs;

■ other business groups.

These are the events you attend with the prime purpose of networking. You go where your customers go (or to meet people who could lead you to a customer).

Informal networking takes place:

■ at the gym;

■ at the golf club;

■ at PTAs;

■ at churches;

■ at social clubs;

■ at parties;

■   on aeroplanes;

■   and absolutely everywhere you come into contact with other
     people.

However, this doesn't mean boring the pants off everyone you
meet, telling them about your wonderful product or service. But it
does mean taking every opportunity to sell – *you*.

After all, to most people, you are the business. I'm sure you've
heard the saying 'People buy people first.'

If people *buy you* then they're much more likely to be interested in
what you do and accept what you say.

How to network

■   **Be prepared**. This applies particularly if you're attending a
     formal networking event such as the chamber of commerce.
     Think about whom you'll be meeting and consider what your
     opening remarks or questions will be. Also think about what
     you're going to say when they question you. (We'll look at this
     a bit closer below.)

     Make sure you have lots of business cards, a small notebook
     and a pen. These should be easily accessible and not involve a
     rummage through pockets or a bag to find them.

> Reminder – *never* go anywhere without business cards

■   **You don't necessarily need to take brochures**. These can be
     sent when you follow up later. A networking event is not a
     place to sell your product or service. (This is not understood by
     the people who have bored the pants off me over the years.)

- **Think about what you're going to wear**. I've seen people rush into a networking event in clothes that look like they've been slept in. If it means having a change of clothes in the office or going home to freshen up – then do it. Remember, the image you present to other people, is the image they'll have of your business. Men should wear a bright tie (not a cheap one) and women should wear something bright. However, remember – business dress, not sexy.

- **Personal hygiene**. Brush your teeth or use a breath freshener. I've met people at networking events whose breath would bring down a rhino at 50 feet. Avoid drinking wine; it can make your breath sour, especially to those who are on a soft drink.

- **Watch out for the perfume**. This applies to both men and women. Strong scents can be overpowering.

- **Name badges**. They'll probably hand these out at the event, but consider having your own produced. They're not expensive to buy and it means you can ensure that what's on the badge is what you want. (Conference organizers often get the details wrong on name badges.) Pin the badge on your right lapel so that it's easier for people to read. The majority of people shake hands with their right hand. As you lean forward to shake hands, it means that the other person can read your badge easily.

- **Go with a partner**. Take a friend or one of your team to a networking event. While you're there, alternately separate and come together. When you see your partner with someone or a group, walk up and let your partner introduce you. Your partner will introduce you using your Sloggo (we're coming to that shortly), it's then easier for you to make more contacts.

Approaching people

I've been attending networking events for over 15 years and I'm still slightly self-conscious about approaching two or three people chatting together. However, I know I'm there to make contacts so I get on with it.

I have never been rejected by anyone and in most cases people are pleased that you've joined them. They also want to network and it saves them the trouble and difficulty of approaching you.

- **Smile, look friendly**. If you look too serious you may make the other people feel nervous.

- **Opening remarks**. These could be 'Hi, I'm Alan – what did you think of that speaker?' or 'Isn't this a great venue, have you been here before?' or 'Did you enjoy your lunch?' Any other kind of opening small talk is good. If you approach someone at the buffet table you could ask them about the food.

- **Don't be negative and don't whinge**. Don't say things like 'What a miserable day' or 'I don't think much of this hotel' or 'I didn't think much of that speaker.'

- **Open with something positive**. Introduce yourself and then ask 'And what does your business do?' Use the person's name and the business name from their badge.

- **Get interested**. If you want to be *interesting* then be *interested*. This is one of the best ways to sell yourself. Look at them and smile; listen and look like you're listening. Empathize with their problems and give them genuine compliments. Use their name but don't overdo it. Find out everything you can about the individual and their business.

- **Don't be dismissive of people**. It's too easy to think 'They're not a potential customer for me' and then switch off. I've been in the situation where someone has said, 'Alan, I don't think I'd be able to do business with you, however I do know someone who'd be very interested in what you do. I'll give them your card.' Of course, you politely ask if it would be alright to contact their friend. Remember – people may not be able to do business with you but they can become one of your unpaid salespeople.

- **Be likeable**. People will only talk about you to other people if they like you. You might have the best product or service in the world but people won't talk about you or your business unless they like you.

- **Keep moving**. Although you want to spend time with people, there comes a point when you'll have found out all you need to know, and established whether you're going to follow up later or not. Resist the temptation to talk too much about your business even if the other person is interested – leave that for another time. You need to move on and meet some more people, after all, that's why you are really there. You could make your exit by saying something like 'It's been really interesting talking to you Mary, I'll give you a call next week with that information I promised and perhaps we can talk further. I need to go and get another drink.' Make sure your glass is empty and theirs isn't, or you'll feel obliged to get them one. You could also say 'I must go and wash my hands' or 'It's been really interesting talking to you John, thank you for your card, I've just seen someone I'd like to talk to, hopefully we'll meet again.'

- **Don't drink alcohol**. Skip the wine and have an orange juice, water or a coffee. Networking is a semi-social occasion but you're there to do business. Alcohol and business don't mix.

- **Get there early**. Your goal is to meet as many people as possible so get there when the event starts. Also be the last to leave. I've made some great contacts as I was walking out the door.

Of course the moment will come when they ask the inevitable question, 'And what do you do?'

This is your moment – your chance to tell people about your wonderful product or service and mesmerize them with your brilliance – *No it's not!*

Remember: when networking your goal is to sell yourself to as many people as possible. The objective is to get them really interested in *you*, eventually bring you business, or tell other people about you. When you start to talk about your product or service, there's a strong possibility that the other person will switch off.

That's why you need a Sloggo – you need to say something that'll grab the other person's attention and make them want to hear more.

A Sloggo (sometimes known as an elevator speech) needs to be:

- a brief description that says exactly what you do and who you do it for;

- a benefit statement that offers value to your customer or client;

- short and punchy – 10 to 20 seconds maximum;

- not glib or yucky;

- variable – you should have different Sloggos depending on who you're speaking to;

- delivered with enthusiasm and energy;

- associated with good feelings – appeal to the emotions;

- something you can use on various occasions: over the phone, on your business cards, brochures, website, e-mail signature or letterheads;

- something that grabs attention and makes the other person want to learn more.

Here are some examples of Sloggos from people in various businesses.

- **A computer or software business**. 'I show companies how to get more out of their computer systems so that they can improve their customer service and get more sales.'

- **A marketing business**. 'We improve a company's image so that they generate more profit from their business.'

- **A financial business**. 'I show people how to save money so that they can have an enjoyable retirement.'

- **A relocation business**. 'We move people's domestic and commercial belongings, with great care and with no stress to the individual.'

- **I would say** 'I'm a professional speaker, I show businesspeople how to motivate their customers, motivate their staff and motivate themselves.'

Write out your Sloggo and practise it until you're comfortable with it and it becomes part of you.

Once you've gained the other person's interest, your goal is to find out about them and what their needs are. There is no point in talking about the features and benefits of your product or service if they are of no interest to the other person.

> *Remember* – You are not selling. You want to find out about the other person, and if there is potential to do business, or if they can lead you to business. If there is, then agree to follow up at a later date by phone or make an appointment there and then.

Follow up your networking

You should have collected lots of business cards at any networking event. These should also be marked with information that'll help you with your follow-up.

When you get back to your desk log all details into your contact list. A product worth investing in is a card scanner. This is an excellent product which makes the job of inputting information so much quicker. There are several on the market. Or download a card scanning app to your Smartphone; again there are several, some of which are free.

- **Do the things you promised people**. If you said that you'd send them information, then do it right away or tell them when you will be doing it.

- **Add them to your newsletter list**. It's important that you get their permission to do this.

■ **Follow up the leads they gave you**. If they gave you any information follow it up quickly. It's also a good idea to let the person know that you followed up their lead and possibly thank them for it.

■ **Make appointments to discuss things further**. Do it the next day while you are still fresh in the other person's mind. A week later and they may have forgotten you.

Be aware; do not fall into the trap of thinking that just because you had a nice little chat with someone and they asked for your business card that they'll do business with you. It may happen but you're going to have to do more.

Keeping in touch

■ Send them your printed or e-mail newsletter.

■ Send them occasional bits of information through the post with a handwritten note.

■ Send them Christmas, birthday, Easter, New Year, Thanksgiving or any other relevant greetings cards (don't send them all or you'll drive them crazy).

■ Send the occasional e-mail with some information that they may find useful.

■ Invite them to an event, particularly where they'll get to mix with some of your other customers.

■ Don't be a nuisance – just keep in touch.

GENERATING REFERRALS

Referrals are an extension of networking. If people like you, or already use your product or service and are totally satisfied, then there's a good chance that they'll recommend you to others. However, that won't always happen; people won't necessarily go around singing your praises to other people, unless someone asks them about you. You can, however, take various actions to improve your chances of getting referrals or word of mouth as some people like to call it.

■ **Ask your existing customers** if there's anyone else they know who could use your product or service.

■ **Ask if it's OK to contact them** and if it's OK to use their name.

■ **Ask them** if they'd be kind enough to refer you to the other person.

■ **Ask if it's OK to check back** and find out what the other person said. (This encourages the person you're speaking to to refer you.)

■ **Offer incentives** such as a free product, a discount or a prize to an existing customer who refers you to a new customer.

■ **Offer a 'finder's fee'** to anyone who finds you new business (or donate money to their charities).

■ **Have a referral form** such as a simple document that you hand out to customers or give away at events or even post to people. It needs to say something like 'Who do you know who could use our product or service?' Then leave some blanks on the form for the details. Mention what the incentive or reward is for them to do this.

■ **Ask existing customers for letters or e-mails of recommendation** so you can use some of their comments on sales letters, your website or brochure.

■ **Listen for referrals** such as a customer's throwaway remark, 'My brother-in-law suffers from the same problems in his business as I do.' You then ask politely about the brother-in-law's business and if it would be OK to contact him. (This seems so simple but many people don't pick up these remarks or do anything about them.)

■ **Thank people for referrals** and when new customers contact you, ask them how they heard about you. (You should always do this so that you can evaluate your advertising or promotional activity.) If they tell you that they've been referred by someone else send a thank you note to the referrer. It'll encourage them to refer more people.

■ **You refer business to them** – it's the old 'I'll scratch your back if you scratch mine' story. Tell people about businesses you'd recommend. If you think they'll do something about it, phone your contact at the business you've recommended. Tell them 'Watch out for so and so who's going to phone or come and see you.' Pass on any details you have, and hopefully they'll do the same for you one day.

■ **Record a video referral** using a small video camera, a compact camera or a Smartphone, all of which have the same facility.

How to promote your business

There are many ways you can promote your product or service, and motivate customers to come to you. You can:

- advertise in national newspapers, local newspapers, trade magazines, consumer magazines and *Yellow Pages*;

- send direct mail;

- hand out fliers;

- sponsor an event, competition or a sports team;

- exhibit at trade shows;

- write articles;

- send out newsletters;

- send e-zines (e-mail newsletters);

- send out a news release;

- run seminars;

- give away or sell branded merchandise.

It's unlikely that you'd want to do all of these; however, we'll look at some of them in more detail.

It is, however, important to remember that, whatever promotional activity you decide to do it needs to be relevant to your business. Always be honest with yourself and ask, 'Will this promotional activity bring more new customers into my business?'

When I first started my business I allowed myself to be talked into advertising in the local newspaper. If I'm honest, I did it to see my name in print – to satisfy my own ego. But it was not the way to bring new customers into my business.

You also have to think of promotional activity as part of a campaign that links together. If, for example, you decide to send out direct mail how will you follow it up? Will you follow up by phone or will you send another letter in a month's time? There needs to be consistency in what you do.

You wouldn't want to do a mailshot this month and then in a couple of months put an advertisement in a trade magazine. If you decide that direct mail is the medium for you, then you need to commit to it on a regular basis. It can take up to seven mailings before a potential customer takes action.

I said it before and I'll say it again, it's vital to measure your activity, you need to ask customers why they contacted you. Are they responding to an advertisement or is it word of mouth? Only in that way will you know how to continue your promotional activity.

GETTING THE MOST FROM ADVERTISING

Whatever you advertise in, you have to ask yourself 'Will my customers read this publication and will they take action having read my ad?'

- **National newspapers**. Read by a huge but decreasing cross-section of the population. If you're inserting a display ad then it would need to be professionally designed, and you'd need to be in it for the long run. It would be expensive and I don't see any small- to medium-sized business justifying the cost. It may suit you better to use the classified advertising in the national newspapers – again, it depends on the type of business you're in. Check out what your competitors are doing and if they are in it, then perhaps you need to be.

■ **Local newspapers**. May be more appropriate for your business, particularly if you only want business from the local area. Again, you must be prepared to consider an ad every day or at least once a week for several weeks. Classified ads may be more suitable for your business, particularly if you have a product or service that people would read the classifieds to find.

■ **Business/trade magazines**. There's a magazine published for almost every business you could think of. They are often produced by trade associations. If, for example, your product or service is used by plumbers and heating engineers, then it makes sense to advertise in their magazine. Use the internet to find the magazine or association you want.

■ **Consumer magazines**. If your product or service is used by the consumer, then this is for you. These again can target specific markets. I know of an image consultant who also does wedding make-up. She advertises her make-up service in wedding magazines. She also, separately, advertises her image service to the mother of the bride in the same magazine. Think about the people who buy your product or service and there's bound to be a specialist magazine that they read.

■ **Magazines last longer**. You'll get more mileage out of a magazine as they tend to be read several times. They mostly come out once a month so people take more time to read and reread them.

Grabbing attention

People skim through newspapers and magazines and they aren't necessarily looking for information on products or services (unless they're reading the classifieds). It's therefore absolutely vital that your advertisement grabs their attention and encourages them to read more. Many ads are designed merely to create awareness of a product or service, however, small- to medium-size businesses need a result.

- **Use words that attract attention in your headline**. The two most powerful words in a headline are 'you' and 'free'. Other great headline words are 'how to', 'new', 'the secrets of', 'amazing', 'breakthrough', 'announcing', 'discover', 'protect', 'facts you' and 'at last'.

- **Don't worry too much about a photograph or a graphic**. A good headline is what you need to grab attention and differentiate you from your competitors. There are several ads in my local paper for plumbers. All but one has the name of the plumbing business at the top of the ad – 'Fred Smith Plumbers'. One ad that caught my eye was the 'Drain Doctor', it made me want to read more. To me one plumber is much like another, however, this one grabbed my interest.

- **Offer something free**. A sample, an hour of your time, information, a drink, a coffee, some food, a place for children to play, a book, an audio or video tape. Offer something that has a high perceived value for the customer but a low cost for you. Remember – you want them to respond to *your* ad not your competitors'.

- **Use simple language**. Get to your point *fast*. Remember, people will only spend a few seconds looking at your ad, so don't beat about the bush.

■ **Offer benefits**. As with your brochure, tell the customer how your product or service benefits them or solves their problems. Don't start sentences with 'We do...', start with 'You will...'

■ **No jargon**. Watch out for abbreviations, jargon, buzz words and technical information. You might understand the language but does the customer?

■ **Don't be boring**. Don't use words like 'quality service' (what does that mean?), 'established in 1862' (who cares?), 'we provide an individual service' (doesn't everybody?). Look at what some of your competitors say in their advertising and do something different.

■ **Touch the emotions**. Make your ad look and sound human, warm and friendly. Perhaps add a name 'Call Jim now for a FREE quotation.'

■ **Use testimonials**. List the names of people and businesses that you've worked with and what they said (with their permission of course).

■ **Call for action**. Your advertisement must prompt people to do something. You must ask them to phone you, come and see you, ask you to see them or place an order – *now*. Make it as easy as possible for them to do that. Provide a free phone number, a freepost address, a simple tear-off coupon to complete, something free or any other incentive for them to take action *now*.

ADVERTISING IN *YELLOW PAGES*

Before you place an advertisement in *Yellow Pages* you have to be sure that your potential customers will look there to find your product or service. Ask your friends and other contacts if they would look in *Yellow Pages* to find a business such as yours. I don't advertise in *Yellow Pages* because my potential clients are unlikely to look there for a professional speaker or consultant. However, there are many services that people do look up in *Yellow Pages*. On any given day, 23% of the population of the United States refers to the *Yellow Pages*. Eighty-four per cent contact a business and 49% go on to buy.

If you feel that *Yellow Pages* is for you then you need a display ad. Eighty-four per cent of people who look at *Yellow Pages* respond to a display ad rather than a listing alone. So you need to ensure that your ad encourages potential customers to phone you first rather than one of your competitors.

People may intend phoning several advertisers in *Yellow Pages* to compare prices and services. However, if they're impressed by the first person they speak to, then they're unlikely to continue phoning around. That first person has to be you or someone in your business.

Think of a service that you might use and look up *Yellow Pages*. Which are the ads that grab your attention first? Why do they do that?

The rules for advertising that we looked at previously still apply. You have to grab the customer's attention and encourage them to phone you first.

You don't want to use up valuable selling space with logos, graphics or photographs because it's more important to get the text right. And as stated above offer an incentive for them to phone you first and *now*.

Using direct mail and sales letters

We hear a lot of talk about junk mail nowadays. Many people will tell you that they dump it straight in the bin. But why do you think so many organisations send out so called junk mail? Because it works.

I dump most of my junk mail just like everyone else, but every so often I'm attracted and respond to something that comes through the mail.

Whatever it is grabs my interest just at the right time. Sometimes it's a mailing I've seen several times and I've been slightly interested; however, there comes a time when I decide to do something about it. (Remember what I said about people having to see an ad seven times before they respond – it's the same with direct mail.)

I'm not looking for a new credit card at present; however, there are thousands of people who are. These people will respond to a credit card company mailing because they want a new card with a better interest rate or their other card is at its limit or they want to transfer a balance.

It has to be said that the average response rate for direct mailing is less than 1% and, as you'll appreciate, the large organizations send out millions of direct mailers.

Small- to medium-sized businesses can have success with direct mailing by keeping it small, focused and personal.

Target the right people – you need to have a good mailing list. The best you can have is the one you've built yourself. You build it with all the contacts you make from your networking and all the enquiry phone calls you receive. (If anyone contacts your business you need to capture all their relevant information. Tell them that you'll add them to your mailing list so that they'll receive all the up-to-date information.)

Buy or rent a mailing list. There are many reputable suppliers (and some not so reputable) who'll supply you with a closely targeted list. If you want the names of transport managers in the food industry in your city, then they could provide it. For consumers, they can supply details of people by zip or postal code, age group, gender, special interests, etc. You could probably get the details of female accountants under 30, interested in fishing and living in a specific area of your city or country. (Not sure why you'd want that, but you'll get the point.)

The product or service has to be appealing. It has to have benefits or problem-solving abilities for the person you're targeting.

■ It must be clear, easy to understand and believable.

■ There must be a call to action.

There are three things that someone will do with a piece of direct mail.

1. Scan it and throw it in the rubbish bin.

2. Put it aside to make a decision later. (However, later never comes, or when it does, most mail will be binned.)

3. Take action – phone the free number, tear off the pre-paid reply coupon or complete the order form.

It's therefore important that your mailing prompts action immediately.

CREATING GOOD SALES LETTERS

You could just send out your brochure but it's much better to personalize your mailing with a well written sales letter.

■ **Personalize.** Using the person's name in a sales letter will give you the greatest success. It is feasible to address sales letters to 'Dear Transport Manager', 'Dear Friend', 'Dear Sir or Madam' or no salutation at all. However, this lessens your chances of getting a response.

■ **You must have a good headline.** You've got to grab the reader's attention as quickly as possible. There must be a reason for them to read on. The same rules apply that you used in your advertising or your brochure, you need to start with words such as 'how to', 'discover' or 'the secrets of...'

■ **Start with an anecdote.** Introduce your message with a short relevant story. For example, you might use something like this if you were introducing a management training programme – 'Seventy per cent of employees don't leave their job they leave their manager!' You would then provide supportive statistics and give details of the cost of staff turnover. You would go on to show how you could reduce these costs and improve productivity through your training programme.

■ **Lots of 'you' and no 'I' or 'we'.** Make each letter sound like you're speaking to that individual rather than to a group of people.

■ **It needs to tell the reader what's in it for them**. How they will personally benefit, how their business will benefit and how their problem will be resolved.

■ **Be believable**. Don't make fantastic claims for your product or service – your letter has to be credible.

■ **Write the letter as if you were speaking to the person**. It has to sound human – warm, friendly, sincere and not too business-like. Read your letter out loud and if it sounds pompous or businesslike then rewrite it. You have to sound like someone your prospect would like to do a deal with.

■ **Appeal to emotions**. Human beings are 100% driven by their emotions so that's what you have to appeal to in any of your promotional materials. Use words such as 'feel'. For example, 'You will feel less stressed when you follow this programme.'

■ **Action**. There must be a call to action so tell the reader what to do now and offer an incentive such as 'Phone now to receive the early bird discount!' or 'Return the enclosed form today to receive your FREE gift!'

■ **Signature**. Signing each letter by hand (in blue ink) will increase your chance of a successful response. Depending on numbers, this may not always be possible so use the best software you can to make your signature look realistic.

■ **P.S.** Include a P.S. after your signature, something that will tease the reader to read the text. People will look at a letter headline first, then scan the bottom of the letter to see who it's from. They'll then read the P.S. and that should encourage them to read the body of the letter, for example, 'P.S. The free report will be sent within two days.' They will be encouraged to read the letter to find out what the free report is all about.

■ **Remember the rule of seven**. One letter won't do it, you'll need to send at least seven over a period of time.

Treat your reader with dignity, respect and courtesy. The trick is in not making a sales letter sound like a sales letter. It needs to come across like a personal message to the individual. If they feel that you understand them and care about their situation then they are more likely to bring their business to you.

USING POSTCARDS

When you have a good mailing list, sending postcards is a great way to maximise the exposure of your product, your service and most importantly, your name.

Postcards are less expensive than sales letters and brochures and less threatening to the customer. They will not automatically think 'Here's some more sales junk.' It doesn't need an envelope and it makes an immediate impact on the customer. It could include a photo on one side and the message on the other.

You could run a postcard campaign whereby you send a pre-printed card to everyone on your mailing list. Or you could use them to send individual, handwritten messages.

Here are some reasons to use postcards.

■ **Updates**. When you introduce a new product or service.

■ **A special event**. A sale or a special promotion, a new branch or a change of address.

■ **Thank you**. You may just wish to thank a client for their business or for something else they've done for you.

- **Seasons greetings**. Wish them Merry Christmas, Easter or Thanksgiving.

- **News**. Something new that's happening in your industry – a new way of doing things.

- **New staff**. When someone new joins your business, tell your customers who they are and what they do. It's a good way to humanize your business.

- **Just to keep in touch**. Postcards are a great way to keep your name in front of the customer because at all times you're seeking to build brand recognition.

Your designer or local print shop can produce these for you and you can also produce them online.

PUBLISHING NEWSLETTERS

This is another great use for your mailing list. You have to accept that there are people who will read your newsletter and there are those who won't. However, it does help to build brand recognition and keeps your name in front of your existing and potential customers. People are also more likely to read a newsletter than a sales letter because they see it as less threatening.

A newsletter lets the customer know that:

- you are an expert in your field;

- you are prepared to give them lots of free advice, tips and ideas;

- you have some new products or services;

- you have a sale or a promotion coming up;

- you understand the customer's industry and their problems;

- you are a human organization with lots of lovely people;

- you are an organization to be trusted;

- you provide great customer service to other organizations.

You can use your newsletter to build a relationship with your customer and you can also use it as a selling tool.

If you only use it to sell then your customers may become tired of it and dump it quickly. However, if you give them something *free*, such as tips, advice, ideas and information, then they're more likely to stay with you and keep reading.

E-mail newsletter

If your mailing list has the contacts' e-mail address then you may wish to produce an e-zine. This has the advantage of being cheaper (no paper or postage) and can be used more effectively to build your mailing list. You provide a facility on your e-mail newsletter for the recipients to forward your e-mail to other people – and so it grows.

There also needs to be a facility on your website where potential customers can subscribe to your e-mail newsletter.

You can simply write your newsletter as a normal e-mail. However, there are several companies who can help you achieve a high quality newsletter. They provide templates and many other features to make your e-mail newsletters look really professional.

You can insert photos, graphics and cartoons as well as text. There is also the facility for customers to order products by submitting their credit card number.

There are several organizations that provide this service; I have been using Constant Contact for years.

USING THE MEDIA

Another way to get business to come to you is to let the media know about you.

Have you ever noticed that when someone is interviewed on radio, television or in the newspapers about a particular subject, it tends to be the same people? You may even be saying 'Why don't they ever ask me?' Well, the reason is that they don't know about you. If they did know that you were an expert on a particular subject, then there's a good chance you'll be asked from time to time.

There are various ways to make yourself known to the media. One way is to write a *news release*. Send the media a news release when you want to announce:

- a new product or service;

- a new marketing campaign;

- a new address;

- new staff or someone's promotion;

- any other newsworthy information about you, your business or your people.

Editors and radio and TV producers receive lots of information from individuals and companies trying to get publicity for their business. However, they need information that is newsworthy, relevant and interesting for their audience.

There are guidelines for writing and laying out a news release – if you don't meet these guidelines then your release will probably get dumped immediately.

A news release needs to include the following points.

- **A contact person**. In the top left-hand corner of the first page put the name and telephone number of a person who can provide further information. If it's your name then that's acceptable, but an editor would expect to see someone else's name rather than the business owner. If you have an assistant, put their name or your partner's name if they work with you.

- **Date**. Put this in the top right-hand corner. You also need to state when the news release can be issued. If it's for immediate release then use those words. You may want it to be released on a particular date – if so, give the details.

- **Headline**. You need a headline that summarizes the story and grabs the editor's attention. Write what you might expect to see in the particular publication or hear someone say.

- **The body**. Write your news release on one page if you can, two pages maximum, with up to 250 words double spaced and a maximum of four paragraphs. Always write in the third person not the first. Make your information exciting and human, think about what would grab the attention of the readers. Include a quotation from a customer if you can; for example 'Fred Smith, Chief Executive of Apex Software said,

"This is the most exciting new product to be introduced to our industry this year!"'

Here are a few other points to consider when writing a news release.

- **It's not a sales document**. This is news information, it is not an advertisement. You don't want words such as 'wonderful' or 'fantastic new service'. If an editor thinks that you're just trying to get a free advertisement then it will be dumped.

- **Think of questions**. Be prepared for any questions you might be asked if an editor phones for more information; you don't want to blow it if you get to this stage.

- **Get a name**. Find out the name of the person to send it to, if it's aimed at the business community send it to 'John Brown, Business Editor, XYZ Newspaper'. If you can't get the name over the phone then, send it to the 'Business Editor' or the 'Lifestyle Editor'. You can usually find the name of the person you want from the latest edition of the publication you're sending it to. If it's for radio or TV, phone and ask 'Who should I send this to?'

- **Media services**. There are media distribution services who will send out your release to all the relevant people – for a fee.

- **PR company**. You could employ a PR company that will do the whole news release for you. They know how to write it and who to send it to. They will also have contacts – journalists, TV editors and producers. They can often get you an interview with them.

WRITING ARTICLES

Another way to get into bed with the media is to write articles on your specialist subject. If, for example, you run a health and fitness centre you could offer an article on diet, nutrition or exercise to a newspaper or trade magazine. They may even ask you to write a weekly or monthly column.

You then become known to the media as an expert on that particular topic. When they need a comment on diet, exercise or a related subject, then you're the person they'll get in touch with.

If you're a health and fitness expert and the subject of 'days off work due to stress' hits the news, then you may be asked to comment, which means more publicity for your business.

It doesn't matter what business you're in, you're bound to have knowledge, skills and information that other people would be interested in.

Here are some points on writing articles.

- Writing articles puts your name in front of potential customers and lets them see how clever you are.

- It's unlikely you'll get paid for an article in a trade magazine because editors know that it's free advertising for you – and you're not going to complain about that.

- You *can* write, although you may think that you can't. If you can talk about your subject then you can write about it – just write as you would talk. If an editor likes what you've written then they may change it to suit their publication. I once sent an article on sales to a newspaper journalist. She phoned me to say how much she liked it and could she change it to suit her newspaper. I agreed and I got my name in print.

■ You may think that everyone knows what you know – well, they don't, so get that article written.

■ Writing articles also encourages you to think about the business you're in, to research and keep up with the latest trends.

You can also write articles and post them to your personal or business blog. Blogs are very easy to set up and shouldn't cost you any money. You just need to post articles regularly or information on other aspects of your business.

Be prepared for the media

As I suggested earlier, you could be contacted by someone from a newspaper, magazine, radio or TV requesting more information about you and your business so be prepared.

Start now to build a media pack that can be sent to any interested person. It needs to contain:

■ a photograph of you produced professionally and making you look good. Get an image consultant and a make-up artist to make sure you look your best;

■ a photograph of your product or your service in action;

■ your brochure;

■ your biography;

■ articles written by you or about you;

- interview questions that you'd be pleased to answer.

Put all this together in a professional-looking folder ready to be posted to anyone who asks. Don't forget to keep it up to date.

Now let's turn to other ways you can promote your business.

BECOMING A SPONSOR

You or your business could sponsor an event, an award, or a contest. Any of these can be done locally and needn't be expensive.

The publicity you receive could be enormous and possibly a better way to spend your money rather than on advertising.

Consider sponsoring the following.

- A sports team – for example, football, hockey or basketball. It could be a professional, amateur or school team. The professional team would obviously want money while the amateur team would want other support. You could buy the team kit with your name on it or get your name on the team bus.

- A sportsperson – a golfer, a snooker player, a gymnast, a judoist, a Karateka or a rally driver. There are lots of sportspeople looking for sponsorship. However, it's important to pick someone who will get you the most publicity (of the positive kind). My local vitamin and mineral store sponsors a cyclist. They promote the vitamin products that help make the cyclist successful; however, they are now selling some accessories for cyclists. (As you'll gather, they get a lot of cyclists in the store, so why not sell them something else.)

- Someone who is about to go and break some kind of record – walking to the South Pole or climbing Mount Everest. Or simply eating more hot dogs than anyone else. If you were in the hot dog business then you could organize your own contest.

- A contest to find the best garden, artist, bowler, cook or hairdresser. Again, it makes sense to promote something that relates to your business. If you're looking for some ideas for a competition, look in the *Guinness Book of World Records* for the biggest, tallest, heaviest or fastest.

GIVING AWAY SAMPLES

One way to get potential customers to come to you is to give away products, your services, your time or other gifts free of charge.

Of course, giving anything away free needs to be controlled; you need to be fairly sure that it'll result in business either now or in the future.

- **Buy two get one free**. Supermarkets use this type of promotion regularly to get you to buy *now*. You could probably use it in your business. For example, 'Introduce two new members this month and your membership will be free for six months' or 'Order a new computer today and the printer is free.'

- **Time**. Almost anyone who provides a service could offer the first hour of their time free with no obligation to buy. Whether you produce a product or a service you could agree to speak about it at an event such as a meeting at no cost. When you do give your time for free, people often feel obliged to reward you in some way, hopefully by giving you some business.

■ **Getting your foot in the door**. Offering something free is a great way to introduce your product or service to a potential customer. There's then a very good chance that they will stay with you and not buy from one of your competitors.

■ **Speciality gifts**. For example, T-shirts, sweatshirts, baseball caps, pens or anything else with your name on it. As well as the person being pleased to receive the gift, you want to give something that will be worn on the street, at the gym or at the golf club. Don't give gifts that people keep in an office drawer or give to their children.

■ **You will get a return**. The psychologists tell us that if people receive something free, whether it is a product, a service or your time, they feel obliged to reciprocate. That's why so many charity organizations include a free pen when they write to you for money. They know that people subconsciously think 'They've given me a pen so it won't take a minute to fill this in and give them a small contribution'.

■ **You must give value**. Anything that you give away must have a high perceived value. If you give away something that the customer regards as rubbish or a waste of time then your product or service will be regarded in the same way. If you give away a T-shirt, make it a good T-shirt that the person will want to wear all the time.

PRESENTING SEMINARS

If you feel that you're a reasonable public speaker, look for opportunities to speak about your field of expertise. You may even decide to run a full-blown seminar.

Organizations such as Rotary clubs, chambers of commerce and business and trade associations are always looking for speakers. They may pay you money to speak but most don't.

This is not an opportunity for you to blatantly sell your product or service and this will be frowned on by the audience and the people who asked you to speak. It's more of a chance for you to present yourself as an expert who provides answers to problems and free information to your audience.

You need to make sure that the audience has a way of contacting you at a later date if they wish. Your flyer or business card on every seat would do the job. You might also wish to tell people at the end of your speech how they can contact you for further information or sign up for your newsletter.

I know an image consultant who runs free lunchtime seminars for businesspeople. She always leaves with a list of people to follow up and some confirmed appointments.

A lunchtime seminar could also grow into a half- or even a full-day seminar. There would need to be a charge for this but think of all the spin-off business. You may even have products that could be sold at the back of the room after the seminar.

And if you want to improve you speaking skills you should join your local toastmasters' club.

This chapter has been about creating a situation where customers will beat a path to your door, and bring other people with them. Let's now look at how you approach them.

4

How to Sell Yourself

HAVE YOU GOT THE LIKEABILITY FACTOR?

Why do you think Barack Obama overwhelmingly won the US Presidential Election? Perhaps it was because of his policies for change, or even the amount of money invested in his campaign. Or perhaps it was his ability to eloquently express the hopes, answers and beliefs of a good chunk of the American people. Some people may even say that Obama was a better bet than his rival, John McCain.

I think it is probably a mixture of all these reasons, and a few more. But more than anything else, I do believe he also has a high likeability factor.

So what's *likeability* got to do with anything? Surely we're going to vote for the policies not the person? Somehow I don't think so. What so many politicians tend to forget is that voters are humans and the thing about humans is that they will always be driven by their emotions, not their logic. We let our heart rule our head all the time. If we decide that we don't like someone then we have a heck of a job believing anything they say. How well our politicians score on the likeability factor is going to influence whether we believe them or not.

Roger Ailes, the communication coach to Presidents Reagan and Bush Snr, wrote 'The silver bullet in business and politics is the like factor. All things being equal, we are more likely to vote for people we feel we like.'

However, so many of our politicians seem totally unconcerned by this. Consider some other public figures who have been affected by the like factor. Bill Clinton came through some difficult situations relatively unscathed because the American public quite liked him. Margaret Thatcher suffered more than she needed because too many people didn't like her. Princess Diana's funeral gave a clear indication of how many people liked her. I don't believe we would have seen the same outpouring of public grief, had that tragic accident happened to another member of the Royal Family.

If your likeability factor is high, votes go up, sales go up and you go up.

But what about the other people in your life, are they likeable? What about your boss, your dentist or your accountant? I get some funny looks when I tell people that I've no idea if my accountant is any good or not. How would I know if he is a good accountant? I'm not competent to judge. I only know that I like and trust him, and that means he'll continue to get my business.

So how do we get this likeability factor if we haven't got it? Or how do we improve it if we have, and what's it all about anyway?

Some commercial organizations still don't quite understand this. The high street banks in the UK were recently criticized in a report that suggested many customers didn't like their bank. One senior manager replied in the press saying, 'We continue to grow our business because our products and services meet customer demand and expectation.' He failed to realize that it's not just about products and services; it's about the human things, like dropping into your local branch and having a talk with the manager. It's much harder to do that nowadays, which is one of the main reasons for poor reports in customer satisfaction surveys.

Likeability is about being human; it's about displaying warmth. Bill Clinton displays warmth, Hilary Clinton less so. Being known as the Prince of Darkness doesn't suggest too much warmth in UK politician Peter Mandelson. Richard Branson has warmth, so did Princess Diana. Nelson Mandela has it; Margaret Thatcher didn't display it in her time as Prime Minister.

Likeability in people will also be measured by their ability to really listen and be interested in others. Likeable people use your name and look as if they care. We like people who have something positive to say and don't whinge. Likeable people empathize with our problems and accept that we may have a different view of the world from them. Likeability is demonstrated by a genuine smile, good eye contact, a sense of humour and relaxed open body language.

Much of our success in life will be determined by our ability to sell ourselves to others. Whether in our personal or working lives people will judge us by what we say and what we do. However, more importantly, this will be influenced by how likeable we are.

YOU ARE THE PRODUCT

We're all in the selling business whether we like it or not. It doesn't matter whether you're a lawyer or an accountant, a manager or a politician, an engineer or a doctor. We all spend a great deal of our time trying to persuade people to buy our product or service, accept our proposals or merely accept what we say.

Most of the time we'll meet with resistance. For example, 'You're too expensive', 'We deal with someone else', 'I don't agree with you' or 'your proposal isn't good enough.'

There are many things that people will say when they resist what you utter; however, how many of these statements are true?

Salespeople hear 'You're too expensive' and they reduce the price. Managers hear 'I'm not doing that' and they resort to threats. Politicians hear 'I don't agree with your policy' and they try to rationalize.

It may just be that the people you're trying to persuade just don't like – *you*.

OK, so they don't necessarily dislike you, it's just that they haven't *bought* you. Before anyone will accept what you say they've got to like you, believe you and trust you. You are far more likely to believe someone close to you than a person you've only known for five minutes.

Just think for a moment about some of the people who come into your life. They could be people you work with, people on television, politicians or religious leaders. How much of what they say is influenced by how you feel about them?

Before you can get better at persuading or influencing other people you need to get better at selling yourself.

Every day of our lives we are selling ourselves, nothing will happen until we are successful at doing that.

When you meet someone for the first time, whether they are a potential customer, client or some other business contact, they'll make a quick decision about you. Psychologists have established that we subconsciously make around eleven decisions about other people within the first six seconds of meeting them. Human resource managers have admitted in surveys to making a decision about a job applicant within the first 30 seconds of an interview, these decisions being made primarily on how the person looked and carried themself. How we look will confirm or contradict what we say. It's therefore vitally important for you as a businessperson to get the other person to *buy* you as quickly as possible.

Here are ten steps to selling yourself.

1. You must believe in the product

Selling yourself is pretty much like selling anything. Primarily, you need to believe in what you're selling. That means believing in *you*. It's about lots of positive self-talk and the right attitude. The first thing people will notice about you is your attitude. If you're like most people then you'll suffer from lack of confidence from time to time. It really all comes down to how you talk to yourself. The majority of people are more likely to talk to themselves negatively than positively, and this is what holds them back in life. It isn't just about a positive attitude, it's about the right attitude – the quality of your thinking.

Successful businesspeople have a constructive and optimistic way of looking at themselves and their work. They have an attitude of calm, confident, positive self-expectation. They feel good about themselves and believe that everything they do will lead to their inevitable success.

'To believe a thing is impossible is to make it so.'

(Proverbs)

Successful businesspeople also have an attitude of caring. As well as caring for their own success they care about other people. They care about their products and their service and they really care about helping their customers make beneficial buying decisions.

Successful businesspeople exude friendliness, modesty and an air of self-confidence. They draw people towards them.

I'm always amazed when I meet certain salespeople during one of my sales training workshops, who come across to the group as egotistical, boring and a pain. The rest of the participants don't warm to these people and it begs the question, what do their customers think of them? I also wonder who employed these people in a sales job in the first place.

Start to believe in yourself and don't let things that are out of your control affect your attitude. You are the product – believe in it.

2. The packaging must grab attention
Like any other product we buy, the way the product is packaged and presented will influence the customer's decision to buy. Everything about you needs to look good and you must dress appropriately for the occasion. And don't think that just because your customer dresses casually, that they expect you to dress in the same way.

The style and colour of the clothes you wear, your spectacles, shoes, briefcase, watch, the pen you use, all make a statement about you.

How you package yourself can also make a huge difference to your self-confidence. Have you ever noticed how confident and self-assured you feel when you dress in something you feel good in; particularly when someone genuinely compliments you? How you dress can have a huge impact on how you carry yourself and project to other people.

There is the famous story about the 1960's pre-election television debates between John F. Kennedy and Richard Nixon. These debates were also heard on radio, which was much more popular at that time. After the debates a poll was taken of how TV and radio audiences had reacted to the two participants. The radio audience voted for Nixon, but the TV audience voted over-whelmingly for Kennedy. The TV audience liked the look of Kennedy better than Nixon; they liked the packaging.

3. Smile and shake hands

There's no need to get carried away, you don't need a big cheesy grin, just a pleasant open face that doesn't frighten people off. I meet so many people at different business functions and some of them look so unfriendly, they scare me to death. Offer your hand, don't wait for the other person to do it. It doesn't have to be a bone crusher, just a warm positive handshake that creates a physical bond. Here's a tip – as you shake hands, lightly touch the other person's forearm with your other hand. Do this quickly but firmly and do it each time you meet this person. It helps to anchor positive feelings about you with the other person and marks you as someone different.

4. Use names

Use the customer's name as soon as you can but don't overdo it. Business is less formal nowadays but be careful about using first names initially.

It never fails to amaze me the number of salespeople I meet or talk to on the phone who don't tell me their name. Make sure your customer knows yours and remembers it. You can do the old repeat trick. For example, 'My name is Bond, James Bond' or 'My name is James, James Bond'.

5. Watch the other person
What does their body language tell you? Are they comfortable with you or are they a bit nervous? Are they listening to you or are their eyes darting around the room? If they're not comfortable and not listening then there's no point telling them something important about your business. Far better to make some small talk and, more importantly, get them to talk about themselves. It's best to work on the assumption that in the first few minutes of meeting someone new, they won't take in much of what you say. They're too busy analysing all the visual data they're taking in.

6. Listen and look like you're listening
Many people, particularly men, listen but don't show that they're listening. The other person can only go on what they see, not what's going on inside your head. If they see a blank expression then they'll assume you're 'out to lunch'. The trick is to do all the active listening things such as nodding your head, the occasional 'Uh-huh' and the occasional question. We are going to take a look at that great sales skill, listening, in just a short while.

7. Be interested
If you want to be *interesting* then be *interested*. This really is the most important thing you can do to be successful at selling yourself. The majority of people are very concerned about their self-image. If they sense that you value them, that you feel that they're important and worth listening to, then you effectively

raise their self-image. If you can help people to like themselves then they'll love you.

Don't fall into the trap of flattering the customer, because most people will see right through you, and they won't fall for it. Just show some genuine interest in the customer and their business and they'll be much more receptive to what you say.

8. Talk positively

Don't say 'Isn't it a horrible day' or 'Business is pretty tough at present' or anything else that pulls the conversation down. Say things like (and only tell the truth) 'I like the design of this office' or 'I've heard some good reports about your new product.'

9. Mirror the customer

This doesn't mean mimicking the other person, it just means that you speak and behave in a manner that is similar to the customer. For example, if your customer speaks slowly or quietly, then you speak slowly or quietly, too. Remember people like people who are like themselves.

10. Warm and friendly

If you look or sound stressed or aggressive then don't be surprised if the other person gets defensive and less than willing to co-operate. If you look and sound warm and friendly, then you are more likely to get a more positive response. This isn't about being all nicey-nicey. It's about a pleasant open face or a warm tone over the telephone.

Before you can start to get down to the process of selling your product, your service or your ideas, then you need to be as sure as you can be that the customer has bought you and that you have their full attention.

How to Become a Powerful Listener

In Chapter 1 I talked about 'new style selling' which is more about listening than selling. The old style salesperson talks all the time; the new style salesperson listens and identifies the customer's needs.

So let me ask you a simple question. Are you a good listener? Now you might believe you're a good listener, but just stop for a moment and think; how would the following people rate you as a listener – your best friend, your boss, your employees, colleagues and even your nearest and dearest? Rather not think about it, eh!

Let me give you some facts and figures about listening that have been established by research.

G. R. Bell established in 1984 studies that adults typically practise listening at no better than 25% efficiency. In 1983, G. T. Hunt and A. P. Cusella reported how well training directors in Fortune 500 companies rated the listening effectiveness of managers and subordinates in their organizations. Ratings averaged 1.97 on a 5-point scale, somewhere between 'fair' and 'poor'.

Other studies suggest that 60–70% of oral communication is either ignored, misunderstood or quickly forgotten. After 48 hours people are likely to retain less than 25% of what they heard in a conversation.

Now I'm sure this makes a lot of sense to you, because one of the most common complaints I hear from managers and employees is 'My manager doesn't listen to me!'

It's also one of the reasons why difficulties arise in our personal life. How often have people headed to the divorce court saying 'He never listens to me!' or 'She doesn't understand me!'

> *'Nature has given us two ears, two eyes, and but one tongue – to the end that we should hear and see more than we speak.'*
> (Socrates)

Listening is a very powerful sales skill and if you want to *make that sale*, then you need to become a powerful listener. Powerful listening isn't about hearing; it's about really understanding the message that the other person is sending and letting them know that you understand and care about what they're saying. Hearing doesn't take any effort. However, listening takes a great deal of concentration and effort. It gets easier with training and practice, so don't give up on me yet.

It's important to understand why listening can be difficult and there are whole lists of reasons why people don't listen well. One of the main reasons is that we can be distracted both internally and externally.

People have the ability to think at around 400–700 words per minute. People talk at about 120–150 words per minute. So in any interaction there's a huge amount of spare brain capacity unused by the listener.

Because we all have so many other things going on in our lives, it's so easy to let our mind wander off and use that surplus brain capacity to think about something else, when someone is speaking to us. We might have personal concerns that pop into our mind such as issues with our partners or children.

Listening can also be difficult if we're tired, bored, in a hurry, confused or can't make out or understand what the other person is saying.

Here are ten key steps to becoming a powerful listener.

1. **Listen logically**. Stay emotionally detached and listen for facts, ideas and details.

2. **Stimulate the speaker**. Nod your head, lean forward, keep good eye contact and concentrate totally.

3. **Make notes**. If relevant, get all the details down.

4. **Shut out distractions**. Change your environment or shut out all distractions in your mind.

5. **Listen between the lines for hidden meanings**. Listen to the emotional meaning of the speaker.

6. **Use your intuition** and trust your gut feeling.

7. **Observe non-verbal clues**. Watch body language, be aware of what people are not saying.

8. **Listen for what people would like to say** but have difficulty putting into words.

9. **Don't pre-judge**. Keep an open mind.

10. **Don't interrupt** or jump in with an answer or solution.

Commit to practising your listening skills every day. Whenever you come into contact with someone, whether in business or socially, really listen to that person. It's like any other skill, the more you practise the better you'll become. (And just think how much you will learn.)

HOW TO TALK WITH ANYONE

Here are some more tips and techniques to help you talk with people and sell yourself.

- **Respect**. I often hear people say 'That person has to earn my respect.' I suggest you give respect to everyone right from the start. That puts you in a positive frame of mind. If, after getting to know that person, you feel differently, perhaps you should try to see the world the way they see it.

- **Smile**. When meeting someone for the first time, hold back the smile for a few seconds. Then when you smile it makes you appear more genuine.

- **Observe**. Watch the person you are speaking to. How are they reacting to you? What does their body language tell you? Match that body language and the tone and volume of their voice.

- **Keep good eye contact**. Don't stare into their eyes and make them uncomfortable. Look away slowly now and again.

- **Focus**. Keep the spotlight shining on the other person. Use the word 'you' more often than you use the words 'I' or 'we'.

- **Knowledge**. Be aware of what is going on in the world. Take an interest in everything. Even if you know a little about a subject, it oils the wheels of conversation. I rarely buy a newspaper, but subscribe to a weekly magazine called *The Week* that summarizes all the articles of interest from newspapers and media throughout the world.

- **Bite your tongue**. It has been said that people are either speaking or waiting to speak. When some starts to talk about something or a place that you know about, resist the temptation to jump in.

- **Listen to the words**. People are either auditory, visually or kinaesthetically driven. They will use words like – 'I like the sound of that' or 'I like the look of that' or 'I like the feel of that'. Echo that language back to them and it will build rapport.

- **Casually compliment**. Slip in a genuine compliment now and again and move on quickly.

- **Say thank you**. Remember your manners and always thank people for a compliment or for something they will do for you. Not 'Thanks' but 'Thank you for the compliment, I appreciate it.'

The time is going to come when you'll have to get to your feet and talk about your business to a group of people. This could be at a chamber of commerce meeting or a Rotary club. Grab every opportunity you can to speak about your business and sell yourself. But you need to do it well, do it professionally, and still show your human side.

UNDERSTANDING THE PS AND QS OF PUBLIC SPEAKING

Which would you prefer – root canal dental surgery without an anaesthetic or a bit of public speaking? According to the people who research these things, most of us would prefer the former.

Public speaking is still one of our greatest fears and it turns grown men and women into nervous wrecks. The mere thought of it turns our tongue to cotton wool, causes our internal plumbing to act up and our kneecaps to start knocking lumps out of each other.

The problem is that public speaking catches up with many of us at some time, both in our business and personal life. You're asked to make a short speech at Fred's 'leaving do'. The organisers of your business club want 15 minutes on why you make 'kafuffle' valves. A potential client wants a presentation on why they should give you the contract.

There are always the confident people who think 'I'm really good at this, lead me to the podium!' but some of these people could bore your socks off and do more for insomniacs than the strongest sleeping pills.

Maybe you'll be lucky enough to have been on a public speaking course. But more likely, when asked to make a presentation, you'll get hold of a book on speaking, start writing the speech, and lose sleep until the event.

Well, there's no need for all of this because help is at hand. All you need to remember are your Ps and Qs. Let's start with the Ps.

Preparation

When you sit down to write what you're going to say, bear in mind who you'll be speaking to. Will they understand what you're talking about; will they understand the technical stuff and the jargon? If in doubt remember the acronym KISS (keep it simple stupid).

To quote Aristotle 'Think as the wise men do, but speak as the common man'.

Make sure that what you say has a beginning, a middle and an end. Think of some anecdotes that help reinforce your story. People think visually so paint verbal pictures for your audience. And always remember, people want to know what's in it for them, so make sure you tell them.

Place

Have a look at the venue before the event if you can. Although this is not always possible, even if you get there just half an hour before the event starts, you can check out where you'll be speaking. Stand at the point where you will deliver from, imagine where the audience will be and check that they can see and hear you. You may wish to place a glass of water where you'll be able to find it.

Personal preparation

Before any speaking event, think about what you are going to wear. When in doubt dress up rather than down. You can always take things off for a more casual look. Men could remove their jacket and their tie. Women could remove items of jewellery.

Part of your personal preparation should include some mouth and breathing exercises. Practise saying some tongue twisters to give your speaking muscles a good workout. Take a deep breath and expand your diaphragm. Then breathe out, counting at the same time, trying to get up to 50 and not pass out.

As part of your personal preparation, write your own introduction. Write out exactly what you want someone to say about you.

Use a large font, double-spaced and ask the person introducing you to read it. Believe me, they won't object and will probably be pleased and impressed.

Poise and posture

When you're called to speak, stand up, or walk to the front quickly and purposefully. Pull yourself up to your full height, stand tall and look like you own the place. Before you start to speak, pause, look round your audience and smile. You may even have to wait until the applause dies down. Remember, you want the audience to like you, so look likeable. Practise this in front of a mirror or your family; I've heard that children make pretty good critics.

Pretend

I'm suggesting you pretend you're not nervous because no doubt you will be. Nervousness is vital for speaking in public, it boosts your adrenaline, which makes your mind sharper and gives you energy. It also has the slight side effect of making you lighter through loss of body waste materials.

The trick is to keep your nerves to yourself. On no account tell your audience that you are nervous, you'll only scare the living daylights out of them if they think you're going to faint. Some of the tricks for dealing with nerves are as follows.

- Get lots of oxygen into your system, run on the spot and wave your arms about like a lunatic. It burns off the stress chemicals.

- Speak to members of your audience as they come in or at some time before you stand up. That tricks your brain into thinking you're talking to some friends.

■ Have a glass of water handy for that dry mouth.

■ Stick cotton wool on your kneecaps so people won't hear them knocking.

One word of warning – do not drink alcohol. It might give you Dutch courage but your audience will end up thinking you're speaking Dutch.

The presentation

This is it, the big moment when you tell your audience what a clever person you are, and have them leap to their feet in thunderous applause. OK, let's step back a bit. If you want their applause then you're going to have to work for it. Right from the start your delivery needs to grab their attention.

Don't start by saying 'Good morning, my name is Fred Bloggs and I'm from Bloggs and Company.' Even if your name is Bloggs, it's a dull, boring way to start a presentation. Far better to start with some interesting facts or an anecdote that is relevant to your presentation.

Look at the audience as individuals; I appreciate that this can be difficult when some of them are downright ugly. However, it grabs their attention if they think you're talking to them individually.

Talk louder than you would normally do, it keeps the people in the front row awake and makes sure those at the back get the message. Funnily enough, it's also good for your nerves.

PowerPoint

And just in case you haven't heard of it, PowerPoint is a software program that's used to design stunning graphics and text for projection onto a screen. As a professional speaker, I'm not that impressed by PowerPoint. I feel that too many speakers rely on it and it takes over the presentation. After all, you're the important factor here. If an audience is going to accept what you say then they need to see the whites of your eyes. There needs to be a big focus on you, not on the technology.

Use PowerPoint if you want to, but keep it to a minimum. Use more graphics than text, and make sure you're the only person pushing the button.

Why not get a bit clever at using the faithful flip chart, lots of professionals do?

Passion

Passion is what stops the audience in their tracks. This is what makes them want to employ you, to accept what you're proposing and make them want you to marry their son or daughter. Couple this with some energy, enthusiasm and emotion and you have the makings of a great public speaker. Just think of Adolf Hitler, boy could he move an audience to action. It's just too bad he was selling something that wasn't to everyone's liking.

Give your presentation a bit of oomph and don't start saying 'I'm not that kind of person.' There's no need to go over the top but you're doing a presentation to move people to action, not having a cosy little chat in your living room.

That's the Ps finished with so let's look at the Qs.

Questions

Decide when you're going to take them and tell your audience at the start. In a short speech it's best to take questions at the end. If you take them throughout your talk then you may get waylaid and your timing will get knocked out.

Never, never, never finish with questions; far better to ask for questions five or ten minutes before the end. Deal with the questions and then summarize for a strong finish. Too many presentations finish on questions, the whole thing goes a bit flat, and you run over your time.

When you're asked a question, repeat it to the whole audience and thank the questioner. It keeps everyone involved, it gives you time to think and it makes you look clever and in control.

Quit

Quit when you're ahead. Stick to the agreed time. If you're asked to speak for 20 minutes, speak for 19 and the audience will love you for it. Remember, quality is not quantity.

One of the most famous speeches ever 'The Gettysburg Address' by President Lincoln, was just over two minutes long.

I can't emphasize enough how important it is to sell *you*. People buy from people and they buy from people they like. Make sure you have the *likeability factor*.

> 'Be who you are, and say what you feel. Because those who mind don't matter, and those who matter don't mind.'
>
> (Dr Seuss)

5

Using the Proactive Approach

We've looked at how to encourage potential customers to contact you and motivate them to buy. But as you know, you can't just sit back and rely on that as your only source of business. There are certain people whom you need to approach. The only way you are going to make a sale is to get face to face with the person who makes the decisions. So let's look at how to do that.

PREPARATION

■ **Find out names**. If you don't know the prospect's name, telephone first to find out to whom you need to speak. Thank the person who gives you the information and call back later.

■ **Write a letter**. Sometimes it helps to write an introductory letter to say you'll be phoning to set up a short meeting. Keep it brief, and don't include brochures or other information; they could give the prospect an excuse for not seeing you.

■ **Plan your call**. Make sure your work area is clear and that you won't be interrupted. Have a pad, a pen and your diary handy.

■ **Get your prospect's attention**. Be clear about what you plan to say and how it will interest your prospect. Work out your opening benefit statement.

■ **Prepare for resistance**. Have a prepared response to reactions like: 'I'm too busy', 'Not interested at this time' or 'In a meeting'.

DEALING WITH THE GATEKEEPER

When you phone your prospect's organization it's highly possible you won't get through initially even if you have their direct number. There's always an assistant, a colleague or voice mail to deal with. This is where dealing with resistance really starts.

■ Always be pleasant and polite. Use the person's name as soon as you know it; be friendly but not overfamiliar. If they say 'This is Mary Smith, how may I help you?', use your prospect's name and your name and say 'Good morning Ms Smith, will you please tell John Brown that Alan Fairweather The Motivation Doctor, is on the phone for him'.

■ If you're asked what it's about, say 'It's about the contents of a letter Mr Brown has received. I'd be pleased if you'd tell him that Alan Fairweather is on the phone for him.' (If, of course, you've sent a letter.)

■ If you're told that your prospect is in a meeting, find out what time they'll be out of the meeting, and ask if that would be a good time to call.

■ Thank the person for their help and say 'I'll call back at 3.30 and look forward to speaking to Mr Brown then. Thanks for your help Mary.'

None of this is easy but persevere, and don't be a nuisance. Always be friendly, firm and courteous with Mary or whoever it is you speak to.

Dealing with Voice Mail

- Give your name, business name and phone number. Speak slowly and clearly and be warm, friendly and businesslike.

- Say what you do. For example, 'We're the people who minimize production time and cost on... I'd appreciate the courtesy of a return call on...'

- You might want to make an appointment to call back. 'I appreciate you're very busy Mr Brown, however I have some interesting information for you' or 'I have a couple of points I'd like your opinion on. I'll call back at 3pm and would be pleased if you'd speak to me.'

- Follow up with an e-mail and make it human.

- Leave your phone number again, speaking slowly and clearly.

Again this is a challenge, but if you sound warm and friendly and that you could be worth talking to, then you'll get call backs.

Always keep customer details handy because when prospects call back they sometimes say 'Hi Alan, it's Fred, I'm returning your call.'

If you made 20 calls that day, you may not initially know who Fred is, so be prepared.

Selling the Meeting

Once you speak to your prospect on the phone you need to do a good selling job to overcome resistance and get the meeting.

Most of the time they're going to say something like, 'I'm not really interested, we already have a supplier, I'm a bit busy at present.'

Always keep in mind that the majority of prospects are reasonable human beings and they have nothing against you personally. There's also a strong possibility that they'll welcome a visit from you if you sound warm, friendly and businesslike. If you sound like you have some worthwhile information to impart and you don't sound pushy or manipulative, then you're more likely to get that meeting.

Plan your call carefully and consider the following.

- **Be poised and ready to talk**. Don't let yourself be distracted while you're waiting to be put through.

- **Greeting**. Speak a bit slower than you normally would, clearly using the prospect's name, your name, and your business name.

- **Courtesy**. Ask if it's convenient to speak.

- **Stand up**. This may help improve your projection and you'll often feel more confident.

- **Smile**. This is another useful tip which helps you come across as warm and friendly. People are much more likely to respond positively.

- **Introduction**. Say what you do and provide a benefit to the prospect.

- **Close**. Ask for a short meeting at a mutually convenient time.

- **Deal with resistance**. Acknowledge what the prospect says, outweigh with a benefit and close again.

- **Don't use the word 'appointment'**. Say something like 'I'd like to arrange a short meeting and get your opinion on a new service we've introduced.'

- **Don't start selling your product or service on the phone**. Only sell the meeting.

- **Don't say you'll send literature**. Say you'll bring it with you.

- **Don't be pushy**. Be persistent and pleasant.

- **Have a fall-back position**. If they won't see you this time then ask if it would be OK to phone at an agreed time in the future and make sure you do so.

- **Confirm the details**. Make sure both parties know what's happening. Remember to say thank you.

- **Confirm the meeting**. Do this in writing by e-mail or letter.

SIDE-STEPPING INITIAL RESISTANCE

Use the *statement question technique* (SQT) to side-step.

The early stages of the call can be challenging if the potential customer starts throwing in negatives. Try not to get involved in lengthy discussions on what are basically excuses. Instead, try to regain control of the call without appearing to ignore what's been said using SQT; make a statement and side-step with a question, turning the negative into a positive. For example:

'We have our own in-house training team' – *'That's good to hear as we always prefer to work with an established team. What kind of training or development do they currently provide for you?'*

'We have no need for consultancy or training' – *'That's fair enough; it sounds as if you're well planned for the future. Out of curiosity, what kind of development processes have you put in place?'*

'We've used consultants in the past and I don't feel we got value' – *'That's a shame, what help were you looking for, and why didn't you feel you received value?'*

'We already use a training consultancy' – *'Fair enough, what kind of development programmes have they helped you put in place?'*

'I'm just about to go into a meeting' – *'I appreciate you must be very busy Mr Smith, what time do you have now?'*

You won't win them all but if you sound professional and pleasant, potential customers are more likely to see you, so don't give up.

The Greeting

You need to say something like:

'Good morning Mr Jones, my name is Joe Brown from Acme Supplies. Is it OK to speak just now?' (Wait for response.)

'We're the people who help businesses like yours cut down their maintenance costs.' (Don't assume that the prospect knows what you do – they may say they do but inevitably they don't.)

'I'd like to arrange a short meeting where I could get your opinions on a new service we've introduced.'

'Would you be free next Tuesday in the morning sometime?' (Always have another time you can offer if this one isn't suitable.)

Once you've written your greeting, say it out loud and listen to how it sounds. You can also work on getting it to sound warm, friendly and professional.

HANDLING RESISTANCE

If the customer says they're too busy, or they don't need what you're offering, or they ask you to send some literature; say something like:

'I can understand that you're busy Mr Jones, and what I have to show you would take about 15 minutes. Would you be willing to take a look at this new service and give me your thoughts? Is Tuesday OK for you or would you prefer another day?'

'Yes, I could send you some literature Mr Jones. However, I have some other material that I'd like to show you and get your opinion. Is Tuesday OK for you or would you prefer another day?'

What you're attempting to do here is make this a relaxed situation. The prospect knows you're trying to sell something and that invokes their natural inbuilt resistance.

Don't always assume that the customer means what they say, and doesn't want to see you. They may be intrigued or interested in new products or services but just don't want the *hard sell*.

PLANNING EACH CONTACT

You may have heard the saying 'Those who fail to plan – plan to fail.'

You don't want to spend too much of your time sitting around planning, because you need to get yourself in front of decision makers and deal with their resistance. However if you're not sure what your objectives are and you don't have some kind of a plan – then you are going to fail. So consider the following and you won't fail.

- **What do you hope to get from the meeting?** Have a clear objective, and write it down. It helps to have a fall-back objective if you find you aren't able to achieve your original goal.

- **How much do you know about the prospect?** It's sensible to have all records to hand of your previous meetings, and any other relevant details about the prospect.

- **What questions do you plan to ask?** Prepare a list of open and closed questions which will give you the information you need, as well as showing interest in the prospect and helping you achieve your objectives.

- **What objections are they likely to bring up?** List all the possible objections – and how you intend to answer them.

- **The presentation.** Anything you say to the prospect has to have benefits for them personally or for their business. Adjust your presentation according to how they answer your questions.

- **The close.** Put together a closing statement and ask for what you came for.

- **Make an impression.** Think about ways to make the prospect remember you.

- **Psych yourself up for the call.** Get yourself in the right frame of mind – the positive attitude that will achieve your objective.

Use this list to prepare an initial customer contact plan. It will give you more confidence and help produce results.

DEALING WITH FIRST THINGS FIRST

Before you meet the potential customer or client, here are a few points to think about:

- **Don't sit down in the reception area**. When the receptionist says 'Please take a seat', *don't*. You don't want to be the crumpled heap sitting in the corner when your prospective customer meets you for the first time.

- **First impression**. You never get a second chance to change that first impression. Make sure your initial impact conveys your positive attitude, warmth, enthusiasm and friendliness. Remember: *the first thing people notice about you is your attitude.*

- **Keep your eyes open**. Take a good look at your prospect and your surroundings.

- **Sell yourself**. We have looked at how to sell yourself in Chapter 4. Remember: smile, shake hands firmly, look them in the eye, use their name and yours and show interest in your prospect.

SUCCESSFUL SELLING MEANS SATISFYING NEEDS

In Chapter 1 we looked at the new style of selling. It's not about launching into a sales presentation and telling the customers how good your product or service is. It's about building a relationship with the customer. It's about helping your customer become more successful in either their business or personal life or even both.

Your customers want more success in their life and they want certain things when they spend their own or their company's money. Remember what was said in Chapter 1; customers want to move towards pleasure and away from pain. For pleasure they want:

- more money – how to get it or how to save it;
- to be liked;
- to have fun;
- to live longer;
- to be happy;
- to be healthy;
- to be respected;
- to be smarter;
- to have piece of mind;
- to have an easier life.

Your success as a salesperson is dependent on your commitment to the customer's success. It needs to be a win-win situation. You need to help your potential customer make decisions that contribute to that success. Your job is to help the customer succeed by understanding and satisfying their needs.

Remember it's not what you want to sell, it's about helping the customer improve or accomplish something by satisfying needs. However, customers won't always tell you what their needs are, and sometimes they're not always aware of them. Individuals have different needs and your job is to identify them.

You do this by listening carefully and with an open mind. You're listening for words and phrases that express desire.

LISTENING TO THE LANGUAGE OF NEEDS

The customer will say things such as:

'I wish...'
'My objective...'
'I want to...'
'We're looking to...'
'I'd like...'
'Our goal...'
'It's important for us...'

If you listen with an open mind to the language of needs, you should not make unwarranted assumptions about what the customer wants and waste time talking about things they're not interested in.

When I was buying a mobile phone I had to listen to a salesman 'banging on' about how this phone could take pictures, handle e-mail, had lots of games and showed video. All I wanted was a phone that I could make calls on and could be used throughout the world.

The simple successful sales call that will minimize sales resistance has four steps and they need to be managed and directed by you – not the customer. Your goal is to reach a mutually beneficial decision that focuses on the customer's needs.

6

Four Simple Sales Steps

This book is designed for businesspeople who need to make sales but are not so keen on selling. That doesn't mean you can just wander into a potential customer's office and have a bit of a chat. You need to have a plan. Your plan should be designed to ensure you obtain the result you want from the meeting and also make you appear very professional to the customer. Follow four simple steps.

1. **The opening**. This is where you exchange information about what will be covered and what you hope to accomplish during the call.

2. **Questioning**. This is the *finding-out* bit where you gather information on the customer's needs.

3. **The presentation**. This is where you provide information about how your product or service will satisfy the customer's needs.

4. **The close**. This is the point where you exchange information about what happens next – how you move forward together.

STEP 1. THE OPENING

When do you open the call?

You open the call when you and the customer are ready to do business, when all the introductions and small talk are finished.

However, throughout the meeting you must keep using the ten steps to selling yourself that are listed in Chapter 4 (pages 98–102).

With some customers you may need only the very minimum of small talk; they may wish to get down to business as soon as possible.

How to open the call

1. **Propose an agenda**. You do this by saying what you'd like to do during the call. You tell the customer what you'd like to accomplish.

2. **Explain how the customer will benefit**. You need to state the value to the customer, tell them what's in it for them and show them how they'll benefit.

3. **Check for the OK**. After proposing the agenda and stating its value to the customer, you need to check that it's acceptable and that it's OK to proceed. You will also want to check if the customer has anything to add.

Here's an example. If you were selling a training course on customer service, you might say something like:

1. **Propose agenda**. 'What I'd like to do today Mr Smith is find out how your telesales team deal with difficult customers.'

2. **Explain how the customer benefits**. 'This will enable me to make a proposal that will improve your customer retention and stop them buying from your competitors.'

3. **Check for the OK**. 'Are you OK with that?'

Another example might be if you were selling computer systems you might say:

1. **Propose agenda**. 'I'd like to talk about your current computer system and how you propose to develop it.'

2. **Explain how the customer benefits**. 'That way, I'll be able to make some suggestions that will address your specific needs and benefit your business.'

3. **Check for the OK**. 'Is there anything else that you'd like to discuss?'

If you were calling on an existing customer you would use the same procedure for opening. You might say:

1. **Propose agenda**. 'The last time we spoke you mentioned that your salespeople weren't converting enough enquiries into orders.'

2. **Explain how the customer benefits**. 'What I'd like to do today is find out how they currently follow up on sales calls. This will enable me to make a proposal that improves your sales conversion ratio.'

3. **Check for the OK**. 'How does that sound?'

Overcoming resistance

The customer may raise an objection at this time and we'll look at how to deal with this on Chapter 7.

However, he or she did agree to see you and they may just be letting you know that they are no walkover.

STEP 2. QUESTIONING

Before you can talk to the customer about your product or service, the two of you need to understand the customer's needs. You ask questions to identify those needs.

As a salesperson, this is the most important skill you can develop. By asking logical questions you'll uncover information about the customer's needs. You need to do it in a way that is comfortable for the customer and probably makes them think about needs they hadn't previously considered. You need to have a clear mutual understanding of the customer's needs. You need to understand what the customer wants and why it's important to them. You also need to be clear on all the customer's needs and their priority.

> 'In selling as in medicine, prescription before diagnosis is malpractice.'
>
> (Tony Alesandra)

Before you start asking questions you need to do a bit of preparation.

Preparation

Once you're clear in your mind what objective you want to achieve from seeing this customer, you can prepare your questions by considering what you already know and what you need to find out.

Ask yourself the following questions.

- What aspect of the customer's circumstances might be relevant?

- What's the customer's job? What are their responsibilities within the business? And, to use a salesperson's acronym, are they the MAN (or WOMAN) (the person with the **M**eans or **M**oney, the **A**uthority and the **N**eed).

■ What challenges do they face in their situation?

■ What is the function of their department or business (mission, structure, policies, processes or problems)?

■ What business are they in?

■ Who are their competitors, their market, customers and suppliers?

■ What questions will you ask to get the information you need, and possibly plant seeds of interest in the customer's mind?

■ How should you structure your questions to identify and uncover the customer's needs?

You question to obtain information from the customer. The amount of questioning you do is dependent on how clear the customer is, how well they explain their situation and how complex it is. The more complex it is, the more questions you'll have to ask.

There are two things you need to do:

■ find out the customer's circumstances;

■ identify their needs.

To do that you need to ask a combination of open and closed questions.

Circumstances

Customers have needs because of their circumstances. The more you understand their circumstances, the better you'll understand their needs. For example:

■ a customer may have a salesforce that is not converting enough enquires into orders;

■ they're about to increase the price of their product or service and they know they'll lose customers;

■ they have a new competitor who is undercutting the price of their product or service.

As discussed above when we looked at preparation, it helps a lot if you can find out as much as you can about the customer's circumstances before you meet. The important thing is to find out how your customer feels about the circumstances. You may know that the salesforce could be getting more orders but the customer may not care. What he or she may be concerned about is increasing the average order value and improving the profitability of the business, not the turnover.

Dig down deep

You need to keep probing to identify the customer's real needs, sometimes known as the DBM (dominant buying motive) or the need behind the need.

Say, for example, you sell computers and you open the sale by saying something like 'Tell me about the kind of laptop computers your salespeople use.'

The customer may say 'We use XYZ laptops, we've had them for a few years and they probably need upgrading.'

You may see this as a buying signal and jump in with a presentation on the wonderful new laptops that you sell. *Resist* this temptation and keep probing.

Say, 'What makes you say they need upgrading?' (This is one of the major skills in effective questioning – you ask a question based on the customer's last statement.)

The customer may say, 'We just need more up-to-date machines which cut down on the amount of paperwork we're still doing.'

Keep digging, for example, 'What do you mean by cutting down the amount of paperwork?'

The customer says, 'Our salespeople are spending too much time coming into the office to print off reports and other paperwork and not spending enough time with customers getting more orders.'

So the real need isn't upgraded laptops – it's an increase in sales.

This is very important to be aware of when you start your presentation because you'll not be selling upgraded laptops – *you'll be selling an increase in sales.*

This may seem like an oversimplified example but I'm sure you can relate it to your product or service. The important thing to identify is what are the real needs of this customer? You'll only find out by asking questions.

> *'Successful people ask better questions, and as a result, they get better answers.'*
>
> (Tony Robbins)

Open and closed questions

I'm sure you've heard of these before, however, even some experienced salespeople have difficulty in using them. You need to use a combination of open and closed questions. Open questions are used to get the customer to open up and respond freely. You might ask:

- 'Tell me what you do at the moment.'

- 'How do you achieve that?'

- 'What are you looking for?'

However, if you use too many open questions then you may lose focus. You'll end up with a whole load of information that doesn't really help you achieve your objectives.

Closed questions limit the customer to a 'yes' or 'no' answer. For example:

- 'Have you ever used a training company before?'

- 'How many salespeople do you have?'

Or the customer may just respond to a choice such as:

- 'Do you prefer in-house training or external?'

Closed questions will help you direct the conversation and they're also useful if the customer starts to ramble. If you use too many closed questions, then the customer may feel that they're being interrogated and start to close down.

Many salespeople overuse closed questions in a mistaken attempt to get information. It's far better to use more open questions; this allows the customer to open up and give you the information you need.

Examples of open questions

To find out more about a customer's circumstances you could ask:

- 'How do your salespeople currently deal with difficult customers?'

- 'Tell me about the new product you've just introduced.'

- 'How do your service engineers currently log faults?'

When the customer answers your question, encourage them to clarify or elaborate:

- 'What do mean by that?'

- 'How do you feel about that?'

- 'Why is that happening?'

- 'What makes that important?'

- 'Please tell me more.'

To find out more about customer's needs you could ask:

- 'What kind of training do you need for your people?'

- 'What would you want your new machines to do?'

- 'What do you expect from your service engineers?'

This style of selling means you need to keep asking questions and dig down deep. (I know I've said it before, but it's so important.)

- 'What else do you expect from this training?'

- 'What other features do you expect from this computer?'

Examples of closed questions

You often need specific information so that you are clear about the customer's needs. You might ask:

■ 'Is sales training more important or would customer service training be more appropriate?'

■ 'How many customers do you lose in a month?'

■ 'Of the three things we've discussed, which is the most important to you?'

You need to be very sure that you've understood the customer, so it's a good idea to keep checking by using closed questions. You're looking for a 'yes' or 'no' answer which will enable you to move ahead. Say something like:

■ 'So what's important is increasing your average order value, is that correct?'

■ 'If I understand you correctly, you need to reduce the amount of maintenance time, is that correct?'

This is what the new model of selling is all about – asking questions and identifying needs. Only when you have identified a need, can you begin your presentation.

> The customer is more likely to buy when they are talking than when you are talking.

STEP 3. THE PRESENTATION

This is where you tell the customer how your product or service meets the need or needs that they have expressed but *those needs and only those needs.* Here's a simple example.

Say you're selling a mobile phone. During your questioning you discover that your customer wants a phone that's easy to use and is also a bit of a technophobe. He also wants to use it when he visits his family overseas.

Only tell him how the phone you are recommending meets those needs.

Do not at this time tell him how this phone sends e-mail, browses the internet and makes coffee. You could kill the sale if you do.

How to present

1. Acknowledge the need. In the above example say something like, 'It makes sense for you to have a phone that is easy to use and can make and receive calls overseas.'

2. Describe relevant features and benefits, but *only* the features and benefits that support the need expressed.

3. Check for acceptance.

Selling the features and benefits

When you talk to your prospect about your product or service, it's important that you talk in terms of their needs. Your prospect may not be remotely interested in the fact that you were founded in 1935 or that you're the biggest company in your field.

Always sell results: people don't buy things; they buy what things do for them.

■ Don't sell a training course – sell the results of that training.

■ Don't sell a television – sell entertainment.

■ Don't sell a bed – sell a good night's sleep.

- Don't sell a holiday – sell enjoyment and relaxation.

Features and benefits are key foundation stones of selling:

- a *feature* is what something is or has, for example, 'Our laptop is compact and lightweight and you can slip it into your briefcase';

- a *benefit* is what the feature can do for the customer, for example, 'This means that you take it with you and use it almost anywhere.'

All products and services have features, but the features on their own won't make the potential customer want to buy, people need to see what's in it for them and that's what benefits demonstrate.

Link phrasing

Link phrasing is exactly what it seems to be – using a phrase that ensures we always link benefits to features, for example:

'This car has side impact protection bars, which means that, if another vehicle slams into the side of the car, they'll take the strain of the impact and massively increase your chances of survival.'

(Of course you would only say this to a customer who has expressed a need to feel safe in his or her car in the event of an accident.)

Check for acceptance

After describing the relevant features and benefits, check the customer's reaction. You don't want to move on until you know that your explanation was understood and the benefits you described have been accepted.

When you check for acceptance, keep in mind that you don't have to check verbally. Usually it's sufficient to make eye contact with the customer and assess his or her reaction to the information you've provided and then to respond accordingly.

If there's an indication that a customer doesn't understand or accept the benefits you mention, ask questions to find out what's on the customer's mind and handle the confusion or concern right away.

If you can't tell whether a customer accepts the benefits you introduce, ask a question such as: 'How does that sound?' or 'Would that be of interest to you?'

If the customer reacts favourably to a benefit, make a mental or written note. When it's time to ask the closing question, you'll want to remember which benefits were accepted by the customer.

Step 4. Closing

If you don't ask, you don't get. The time comes in every sales call when you have to find out if the potential customer is going to buy or move to the next step.

This chapter includes dealing with sales resistance and if you haven't had any up until this point then you will certainly get it now. However, if you have successfully dealt with sales resistance previously, then you need to proceed and close the sales call or visit.

To close a sales call you:

1. Review the previously accepted benefits.

2. Propose the next steps.

3. Check for acceptance.

For example:

■ 'As we've discussed, after this training programme your salespeople will be able to take more orders over the phone so increasing your sales and cutting your costs.'

■ 'If we can agree some dates today then we can move ahead with the training next month.'

■ 'Is that acceptable to you?'

However, you will encounter sales resistance, or objections, and that's the next step.

7

How to Deal with Resistance

As described earlier, there are many reasons why you may encounter sales resistance. Even if you have made an impact on the customer, built excellent rapport and made a professional presentation, you may still experience resistance.

Sometimes you have to deal with customers who don't have a particularly strong interest in talking to you. They don't necessarily have objections, or are resistant to what you have to say; they are merely *indifferent*. They may say:

- 'We upgraded our computers last year and they seem to be doing the job.'

- 'Sorry, we're not looking for help in that area at the moment.'

- 'We have an internal training department and it meets our needs.'

- 'My mobile phone does all that I need it to.'

When a customer expresses *indifference*, there are three steps you can take.

1. Acknowledge the customer's point of view.

2. Request permission to ask questions.

3. Question to create customer awareness of needs.

ACKNOWLEDGING THE CUSTOMER'S POINT OF VIEW

When you have a potential customer who is satisfied with things as they are, they may be concerned that you'll try to sell them something they don't need. You can reassure the customer that this is not your intention by conveying that you understand and respect his or her point of view. You might say:

- 'I appreciate that you're not experiencing any problems at present.'

- 'I understand that you're happy with your present supplier.'

- 'You're the best judge of how your current system is working for you.'

REQUESTING PERMISSION TO ASK QUESTIONS

After acknowledging the customer's point of view you ask permission to ask some questions. What you're doing in a short period of time is finding out if there is a reason for you and the customer to continue talking now, or at some time in the future. You are also reassuring the customer that you aren't trying to apply any pressure.

As with any other statements, you want to state the value to the customer of proceeding and also check for acceptance. You might say:

- 'If you'd be willing to spare a few minutes, I'd like to find out a little about how you use your computers. We've worked with many businesses similar to yours and there may be things we've learned that could be of value to you. Would that be OK?'

■ 'I wonder if I could ask you just a few questions about how you produce this product. Even if you're satisfied with your current supplier, we might be able to find ways in which we could help you at some future date. Do you have a few minutes?'

■ 'You're in a market that has a tendency to change rapidly. If I could ask you some brief questions about your long-term plans, we might be able to identify some ways that my company could be of service in the future. Does that sound reasonable?'

QUESTIONING TO CREATE A CUSTOMER'S AWARENESS OF NEEDS

Once you've acknowledged the customer's point of view and requested permission, you ask questions. Your purpose in asking questions is to build the customer's awareness of things that he or she might want to improve or accomplish – and that you can help them improve or accomplish. You question to:

■ explore the customer's circumstances for opportunities and effects;

■ confirm the existence of a need.

Since indifferent customers don't have any needs to tell you about, you can't start questioning about their needs. You can, however, probe into the customer's circumstances, which may in turn reveal opportunities. For example, if you sold a laptop computer which was light and compact with a built-in printer then you would ask specific questions that would indicate a problem that could be addressed by your product. You might ask:

■ 'How often do your salespeople travel?'

■ 'What kind of work do they do when they are away from the office?'

■ 'What kind of difficulties, if any, do they encounter doing this work?'

If the answers to these questions indicate that the customer's salespeople do travel frequently, do have to prepare proposals and presentation materials while away from the office, and do have difficulty because they don't have easy access to computers and printers, you've determined that an opportunity exists.

When you suspect that you'll encounter resistance through indifference, it's best to identify possible opportunities you can ask about before calling on the customer.

Exploring the customer's circumstances for effects

Once you've established that the customer's circumstances could be improved by your product or service, you want to explore the effects on the customer of leaving things as they are.

To determine the effects, you can ask about the customer's feelings or opinions regarding the consequences, impact, results (or lack of results) caused by the condition or problem you've identified. The effects can be in the present or projected into the future. You might say:

■ 'How do you feel about that situation?'

■ 'How does that affect their productivity?'

■ 'What impact will that have on their motivation in the long run?'

■ 'How serious a problem is that?'

Questioning about effects helps you in two ways. It gives you a sense of the importance of the condition or problem in the customer's eyes. It also heightens the customer's awareness of the consequences of leaving things unchanged.

Confirming the existence of a need

The next step is to find out if the customer wants to do anything about the condition or problem you've uncovered. In other words, you want to find out if the customer has a need.

Just because the customer recognized a condition or problem and is aware of leaving the things unchanged, you can't be sure that the customer has a need unless he or she expresses one. To confirm the need, use a closed question.

■ 'Is that a problem you'd be interested in solving?'

■ 'Would it be important to do something about that?'

■ 'Would you like to find a way round that?'

If the customer says yes, you can go ahead and make a benefit statement. If the customer says no, then at least you've created an awareness of a condition that might be important one day – and one that you can address.

PINPOINTING OTHER REASONS FOR RESISTANCE

At any time in the sales call the customer may offer resistance, voice an opinion or express reluctance to make the commitment you're looking for.

There's no need to feel uncomfortable when customers voice concerns, it's just one of the ways they express their needs.

Generally speaking, there are three types of concerns.

1. Dealing with doubt

When you make your presentation, customers sometimes doubt that your product or service has the features or will provide the benefits you've highlighted. They may say:

- 'I've yet to see a built-in printer that produces quality documents.'

- 'A laptop computer that holds a charge for 100 hours sounds too good to be true.'

How to deal with doubt

A customer who is sceptical needs reassurance that your product or service will provide the benefits you have described. You need to:

- acknowledge the concern;

- offer relevant proof;

- check for acceptance.

Acknowledge the concern

When you respond to any concern it's important to let the customer know that you understand and respect it. You might say something like:

- 'I appreciate that you'd want to be certain of something as important as this.'

- 'Given your previous experiences, I can understand why you'd ask that.'

Offer relevant proof

Say you'd told the customer that your laptop would hold its charge for 100 hours and the customer expresses doubts that this is possible.

First acknowledge, then you might say:

'Here's an article from *Computer* magazine. The table on page 48 reviews the performance of ten laptops. As you can see, ours was shown to provide 100 hours of charge, far higher than any other laptop.' Make sure the proof is relevant to the doubts raised.

Check for acceptance

After offering the proof, check to see if the customer accepts it. Say something like 'Is that acceptable to you?'

2. Dealing with misunderstandings

Sometimes concerns arise because the customer has incomplete or incorrect information about your product or service.

To use the example of the laptop computer again the customer may say: 'I don't think a laptop is any use to me, the batteries don't last very long for the work I do and I really need to plug into the mains.'

If the customer had previously expressed a need to work without access to electricity, you would have outlined the benefits of long battery life in your presentation. Since he didn't express the need and assumed you couldn't satisfy it, the need has surfaced as a concern.

Resolving a misunderstanding

■ Confirm the need behind the concern. 'So you need a laptop that will stay charged long enough to complete the work you do.'

■ Acknowledge the need. 'I can understand that this would be important in your work.'

■ Describe relevant features and benefits. 'This laptop has a battery that will provide full power for 100 hours.'

Check for acceptance, for example say 'Is this something you would find useful?'

3. Coping with shortcomings

Any recommendation you present to a customer reflects your best efforts to address the customer's needs. However, every product and service has its limitations and you can't always satisfy all of a customer's needs.

When a customer has a complete understanding of what you are offering but is dissatisfied with the presence or absence of a feature or benefit, then you're dealing with a shortcoming, a need you can't satisfy.

Resolving a shortcoming

A customer whose concern is based on dissatisfaction with what you offer (or don't offer) has to weigh the importance of the needs you can satisfy against the importance of the needs that you can't.

To help the customer make this assessment you do the following.

■ **Acknowledge the concern**. 'I can see why you would like this computer to have a built-in webcam.'

■ **Refocus on the bigger picture**. You now want to put the drawback in perspective. You might say, 'Do you mind if we take a few minutes to review some of the other factors we've discussed?'

■ **Outweigh the drawback** with previously accepted benefits. You can sometimes outweigh a drawback by reviewing the benefits the customer has already accepted. You might say, 'We talked about your need for a powerful laptop that was light, slim, with a large memory and the ability to work for long hours without recharging.'

When you select benefits to review, it's best to use those that meet the highest priorities of the customer. Also include benefits that address the dominant buying motive and particularly, benefits you know your competitors can't provide.

Check for acceptance

You might say: 'In light of your overall needs for a laptop computer and the ability of our model, how do you feel about proceeding at this time?'

Summing up

Dealing with customer resistance is the hardest part of the sales process and it is the basic reason salespeople have jobs. The right attitude in conjunction with a skilful presentation will minimize sales resistance. However, you are dealing with a complex human being who may not understand what you've told them or may be prejudiced about what you offer. Using skilful techniques will improve your sales success so that both you and the customer benefit – think win-win.

I wish you every success.

Index

About the author

Alan Fairweather, The Motivation Doctor, is a dynamic speaker who has been motivating audiences from around the world for the past 18 years.

If you would like to find out more about Alan, please email him at:

askalan@themotivationdoctor.com

Or check the websites:

howtogetmoresales.com
themotivationdoctor.com
managedifficultpeople.com

Alan's previous two books are available throughout the world from your local or online bookstore.

How to be a Motivational Manager

How to Manage Difficult People